EXTRAORDINARY TEACHERS

EXTRAORDINARY TEACHERS

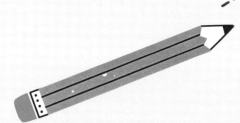

Stories from Everyday Heroes!

Foreword by Dan Shutes

ROCK POINT

Contents

Foreword

BY DAN SHUTES

I can feel the pit in my stomach. My heart rate rises ever so slightly as I anticipate the sound of the whistle . . . I am standing at the end of a mile-long corridor as I wait for the controlled chaos to ensue. The whistle finally blows, and the stampede-like sound gets closer and closer until I am eventually surrounded by hundreds of students pouring down the hallway to their classrooms.

The first scene of each school day has always reminded me of the opening kickoff at a football game—without the opposition trying to hit you as hard as they can, of course. For me, however, the feeling in my stomach is always the same. There is an anxious excitement to it all that has only ever been replicated in my life through sports.

I teach fifth grade at Paw Paw Later Elementary School in Paw Paw, Michigan, and, as you might be able to guess, I am also a coach. My dream to become both a teacher and a coach started back in high school when I was playing basketball my junior year. Part of being a member of the varsity team required each player to oversee and help coach a youth basketball team on Saturday mornings. I vividly remember how much joy these kids had playing and learning from us high school guys. I will also never forget how much fun I had spending Saturday morning with youth athletes. Those Saturday mornings lit a spark for me, which inspired me to pursue a career in education.

There were also several impactful individuals who led me on my path to becoming a teacher. I can still hear my second-grade teacher, Mr. Coleman, holding my classmates and me accountable for having messy desks—not knowing at the time that he was trying to help us understand the importance of doing the little things right. I can still see

Mrs. Tomlinson in her classroom rocking chair reading from *The Indian in the Cupboard* each day after recess—not knowing at the time that she was helping a reluctant reader appreciate a good book. I can still see how easy Mr. Bingaman, Mr. Awe, and Mr. Wagner made it look to relate to a bunch of middle school kids who thought they were too cool for school. I can still hear Coach "Pitro" and Coach Gernon motivating my college team to be the best version of ourselves on and off the field. I'll never forget Coach Gowen blowing his whistle as we ran sprints for wearing different colored socks with our football uniform—not realizing that he was teaching us that individual players aren't more important than the team. And I can still hear Mrs. Nemecek's calm words of encouragement during my teaching internship.

I am now in my ninth year as a fifth-grade teacher, and over four hundred and fifty students later, I can safely say that this job has changed my life. In the fall of 2014, when I started my teaching internship in the same school where I currently work, I remember being led down a long hallway by Mrs. Nemecek, my internship coordinator. At the end of the hall, she stopped at a classroom door, looked me in the eye, and said, "This is you . . ." As I walked through the door into the fifth-grade classroom, I felt the eyes of twenty-five students immediately find their way over to me. They felt like laser beams. Without making eye contact with any of the kids, I walked across the classroom to shake the hand of Mr. Vanderburg, my mentor teacher. Then it was time to formally introduce myself to the class in the form of a short slideshow I had made. I'll never forget fumbling around with the USB flash drive and the computer due to shaking so badly, but as soon as I spoke, everything changed. I didn't stammer over one syllable; I didn't mumble through my words. I didn't shy away from the reality that I was now living in. I got through my introduction in about ten minutes and took a seat in the back of the room. My first thought as I gathered myself at the back desk was, "Why did that feel so easy?" I was a little confused at that moment considering my heart rate was still through the roof. Up to that point, I had very little classroom experience; I was trying to figure out how I hadn't messed up my introduction in front of a live audience of ten- and eleven-year-olds. I recall comparing the ease with which I spoke to the ease of playing sports, and in that moment, I knew I was going to be OK.

I knew right then and there that this was exactly what I was supposed to be doing with my life.

I have learned so many valuable lessons from the kids in my classroom.

During the early part of my teaching career, I always felt overwhelmed with the curriculum, lesson plans, management of daily schedules, meetings, emails, parent communication—all of the "busy work" if you will. Yes, these are all important aspects of the job and require a lot of attention on a daily basis, but I have realized that being a teacher is about so much more than these tasks. The longer I have been a teacher, the more obvious it is to me that kids, just like adults, long for human connection. Kids want to be seen; they want to know that someone outside of their family is in their corner cheering them on. They want to be cared for, and they want to enjoy themselves while they're at school. These are now my core beliefs and the foundation I try to build on each school year.

By all means, I want my students to achieve academic success and growth, but that means very little to me if they don't see school as a place where they want to be. If my students can add two fractions together but don't know that I care about them as people, I have failed. If my students do well on a standardized test but have not developed empathy for those around them, I have failed. If my students can name all fifty states but cannot stand up to a bully, I have failed. I've always said that this job is deeper than what can be printed and shown on paper. In my opinion, this job is about people, not about numbers.

The longer I have been a teacher, the more I realize that my students don't come to school on a level playing field. Some kids come to school with a belly full of food and fresh clothes, and others don't. Some kids come to school having gotten a good night's sleep, and others were up all night because of an argument between two adults. Some kids come to school to learn, while others come to school to be cared for. Some kids arrive at school on time, and others are always late because they are responsible for their siblings each morning. The stories could go on and on, but they all have one thing in common: They have made me a more empathetic teacher and person. It's funny how teachers spend so much time putting their hearts and souls into their students, and, yet, the students always seem to teach us adults even more.

In my years as a teacher, I have learned so many valuable lessons from the kids in my classroom. One would expect the opposite . . . I'm the teacher, right? I'm supposed to be teaching valuable life lessons to the kids, not the other way around, right? While I think I can safely say that I have done my best to do just that, you'd be surprised at just how much kids can teach you in return.

My nine years as a teacher has humbled me and taught me patience. It has taught me the importance of not making assumptions about people. It has taught me that there is always more to a child than meets the eye. It has taught me the importance of being a positive role model for a child and helping them believe in themselves. Teaching has taught me the power of relationships, and, most importantly, it has taught me that the mental health of a child will always be more of a priority than the result on some test.

There is always more to a child than meets the eye.

Now, what if you could dive into the mind of any teacher at any given time? What would you see or hear? Do all teachers have the same philosophies and beliefs? What has been the most impactful experience of their career? Would our stories echo one another? *Extraordinary Teachers* is an attempt to answer those questions. Teachers in every single state, in every single county, and in every single school have a story to tell. While it's impossible for any book to highlight every impactful teacher, this one gives readers a glimpse into the journey of thirty educators from across the United States. This collection of transcribed interviews offers an opportunity to gain perspective through the eyes of others—an opportunity to see what many different educators are seeing, hearing, and experiencing in their own classrooms.

Reading these teachers' stories has reiterated for me that not all teachers share the same philosophies and have the same experiences, and that's OK. Teaching is not a one-size-fits-all profession. Educators do not have the same daily experiences and do not see this job through the same lens. Everyone's journey to becoming an educator has different peaks, valleys, twists, and turns. I think this book is a great reflection of that fact. Ultimately, these words motivate and educate—they represent how teachers connect, support, inspire, and nurture their students.

Everyone's journey to becoming an educator has different peaks, valleys, twists, and turns.

A point that comes up repeatedly in these testimonies is that teaching is deeper than the numbers. Teaching is deeper than what the test scores say; it's deeper than the data, the buzzwords, and the catchphrases. It's deeper than curriculum, evaluations, PLC (Professional Learning Community) meetings, and the like. Education is and always will be about the kids and the impact a teacher can have on their lives. I think you will come away from these pages with a better understanding of what teachers see, hear, and experience each day. There is certainly hope in knowing that there are teachers all over the country who truly care about their students and their well-being.

I'll close this by taking it one step further: as a teacher myself, I want you, if sitting on the fence, to be inspired to go into education yourself. I will never forget the aforementioned people in my life who inspired me to chase my dream of becoming a teacher. I hope this book can push someone else toward doing the same. I hope that every reader who makes it cover to cover can sit back and realize that teaching just might be the most important job in the world.

DAN SHUTES is a fifth-grade elementary school teacher and baseball coach at Paw Paw Later Elementary School in Paw Paw, Michigan. He has amassed millions of followers on TikTok (@danshutes) posting videos about the joys and challenges of teaching and has caught the attention of national media, including Today.com, People.com, and *The Kelly Clarkson Show*.

While they may not reach the exact bars we set, they will strive to improve and they're going to keep reaching.
—LIZ SHERMAN

HOW

do you get a class full of giddy kindergartners to settle down? Or convince a group of high school students that classics are worth reading? How do you get yourself back in the classroom after a rough day? How do you convey how much teachers need their community's support?

Motivation. Extraordinary teachers harness it for themselves and one another, even as they instill it in their students. The specific tools they use can vary widely, from games and pep talks to rhymes and first-hand experiences. Though their toolboxes might be huge, their tools share common themes. Teachers use humor, patience, imagination, empathy. They take the time to forge connections with their students, to see what lights the spark of motivation for each kid, and then they fan the flames. They do the same for each other—extraordinary teachers share their stories with one another with humor and empathy. It's often their connections with one another that motivate them to keep going.

They Motivate

Changing the Game: Finding Motivation

Erin Gruwell *and the* Freedom Writers

Erin Gruwell walked into her first classroom in Long Beach, California, in 1994, idealistic and ready to dive into great works of literature. The students she met, however, were considered by others—and worse yet, believed themselves to be—"unteachable." In a community facing gang violence, poverty, food insecurity, crime, and more, school wasn't a priority for kids; survival was. How could she motivate them to read stories that they couldn't relate to?

Mrs. G scrapped her lesson plans and instead made it her job to learn about her kids. She provided each of them with a journal and told them to write and rewrite their stories. At the same time, they read books by kids who had done the same: Anne Frank and Elie Wiesel during the Holocaust, Zlata Filipović in Bosnia. Soon, the students began believing in the power of story—and most important, the power of their own stories. Mrs. G's students' work was eventually published in a book that became a number-one *New York Times* bestseller. Their story was also turned into the 2007 movie *The Freedom Writers*.

John Hunter *and the* World Peace Game

How do you get fourth graders interested in the world's political, economic, environmental, and military complexities? For teacher John Hunter, the answer was to turn it all into a game. To play, students become countries. To win, they must figure out a peaceful solution to problems from political upheavals, to famine, to environmental disasters like oil spills.

According to the rules he developed, Mr. Hunter can't intervene. He can only ask questions and prompt kids to think through what effects their actions could unleash. Mr. Hunter found that kids could not only grasp complex global issues, but that they were also great at adapting and changing strategies. More often than not, players found that cooperation is the best solution.

Filmmaker Chris Farina asked Mr. Hunter if he could record students playing the game. The result: the 2010 documentary *World Peace and Other 4th Grade Achievements*, which won awards at film festivals and was eventually screened at the United Nations, where generals met with nine-year-olds to talk about peace. The World Peace Game is now played around the world.

Larry Abrams *and* BookSmiles

After a conversation with one of his high-school seniors, English teacher Larry Abrams realized that sometimes the only barrier to motivation is access. Mr. Abrams asked one of his students what she was reading to her child, and she said nothing—she didn't have baby books. The conversation made Mr. Abrams think about "book deserts"—places without easy access to books.

With a simple call to friends, Abrams yielded a flood of donated books. Seeing the joy on parents' and students' faces was all it took for him to want to do more. Now Mr. Abrams runs BookSmiles, which accepts donations of gently used children's books and donates them to kids and schools in book deserts. They've donated nearly two million books since they were founded in 2017.

Elevating Each Other

Ms. Liz Sherman

MICHIGAN

ELEMENTARY SCHOOL
SPECIAL EDUCATION

It makes the world so much better if we can just keep elevating each other.

My passion for education runs deep: I'm a third-generation teacher. My youngest brother, Bradley, has intellectual disabilities and is autistic. Bradley had an amazing elementary school where he found a group of kids who were super protective and supportive of him, and I thought, *Yes, they just needed to know Bradley to love him.* I wanted to emulate that and create that type of community and culture. I also saw what he went through in navigating the education system—and what my parents as well had to go through—and I wanted to make it better. So I went into education, specifically special education. It's close to my heart.

One of the bigger obstacles to overcome has been undoing myths about what disabled children are capable of doing and achieving. Sometimes people have the misconception that a student with a disability can't learn or that their cognitive abilities might make it difficult for them to learn a certain type of content. I set high expectations for every child.

For example, I once had a second grader who only knew two letters of the alphabet and I was told they were unable to do many things. This student believed they'd never be able to read. I told that kid, "It's not true. You're gonna do it, and we're gonna get there." There was a lot of resistance for the first three months. I kept affirming them, building them up, being proud of any small amount of progress. Eventually that child started seeing that they were making progress too.

Everybody's progress is going to look different and it's going to look different every day. But by the end of that school year, that child was reading decodable books, books with digraphs and blends. They were feeling that confidence, and then they were telling the other kids, "Be quiet. I'm trying to learn." That took months, but I knew it wasn't going to be an immediate thing. It takes time to build trusting relationships. For me, building kids up comes naturally—I like being a cheerleader for people in general. I think there's room for everybody, and I have this "Let's all cheer each other on" type of mentality.

Building that relationship starts at the beginning of the year. I make students fill out a survey asking about all of their favorite things, including what they're worried about. It's not just, "What's your favorite color? What's your favorite ice cream flavor?" It's also, "If there is one thing that you wish you knew, what would it be? If there's one subject that sometimes scares you or makes you frustrated, which one is it? Why is that?" It helps me understand them and to sort of help unlearn whatever it is or make it easier.

Again, I might have a child who, from the get-go, says, "I don't like reading. I can't do it. I think it sucks, so, I don't care to do it." And I say, "Got it. My goal this year is for you to just think it sucks a little less."

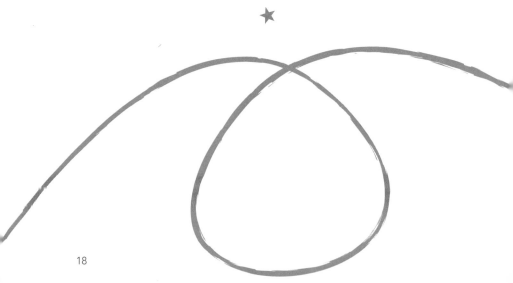

Students nowadays, I feel, are even more socially aware of what's going on. Some kids are concerned about coming to my room, and they ask why. I tell them, "Oh, you just need extra help with something, and I have different strategies and tools we can use." When they understand that, they're more willing. They think, "I just learn differently. Everybody learns differently. So what? We get to come to a cool room instead."

I think we can have a more inclusive world and education system by being empathetic and communicating a little more about our worries, our fears, and our misconceptions. Holding high expectations for all students is crucial; while they may not reach the exact bar we set, they will strive to improve and they're going to keep reaching. It makes the world so much better if we can just keep elevating each other.

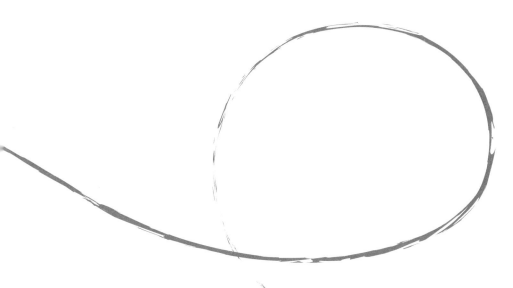

Celebrate It and Recognize It

Ms. Nancy Cheng

CALIFORNIA

FIFTH GRADE
GENERAL EDUCATION

If you don't know how to work with others and respect them and treat them in a kind way, then I failed as a teacher.

I love kids, but my second passion is art. My goal is to integrate art into everything I do, whether it's science or math or English. I've always found art to be very therapeutic. My family and I emigrated to the US when I was ten. I didn't speak any English, so to express myself and feel any self-worth, I created art. For me, it was one way to really show what was in my head. I know not all of my students learn the same way; they don't express their capabilities and their knowledge the same. But when I bring art into their lessons, I can reach those kids who are not great at reading and writing.

With kids, there's never a dull day. I feel like my students keep me young. I just love seeing the world through their eyes. Sometimes when they say something, I think, *That's so silly.* And then I think about it more and I realize, *You know, that* does *make sense.* They help me see everything in a different way. It's my twenty-seventh year teaching, but I'm still learning so much from them because they bring fresh insight to everything.

I also feel like I have such a big impact on their lives, not just academically, but in social-emotional learning, character education, and life lessons. While I teach in a very academically driven area, I tell my students all the time, "Hey, even if you're getting straight As and a 4.0, if you don't have interpersonal skills, if you don't know how to work with others and

respect them and treat them in a kind way, then I failed as a teacher."
We always talk about the importance of that over academic excellence.
"Hey, don't take this for granted" or "What is the value of this lesson?"
I look for those moments.

I came to America when I was in the fifth grade, and I was impressionable
and really needed guidance in so many ways. Fifth grade is the sweet
spot for me. They're still so innocent and sweet and naive, but yet very
independent. I feel like this is my way of giving back and my way of being
there for my students the way that I wish somebody was there for me.

Something that I tell student teachers is to never compare yourself to
anybody. But always do your personal best. I mean that for teachers and
students and everybody. I have students who will start out performing
way below where they should be in terms of standards. Lots of parents
and teachers will compare and tell kids, "This student is at the ninety-
ninth percentile and you're at the eleventh percentile. We've got to get
you up." Instead of packaging it that way, we should tell them, "Hey, you
were at 10.5 before—you made progress." Even if it's small progress,
if we celebrate it and recognize it, they realize, "I am improving." Build
them up with a lot of little pep talks—"Let's celebrate this progress.
You're working so hard, and I know you're growing, and I appreciate you.
You're amazing." Those little pep talks will get them thriving.

When you encourage students in those little ways, they throw it back at
you. This year I had two students who had such severe anxiety when it
came to speaking in front of their peers. At the end of the year, they still
had a difficult time, but when we looked back, I was able to say, "Do you
remember when you used to hide or go to the bathroom every time you
needed to talk? And you did an amazing job." Then sometimes they'll say
to me, "Ms. Chung, you did a really great job." They'll compliment me. If
you share that positivity, they give it back.

A lot of teachers who share their ideas online are taking their teaching and their knowledge to a greater audience. There's an amazing community of teachers on social media who share the latest trends and the best ideas. Whenever I share even an old idea that I've been doing forever, it can reach such a huge audience. I have so many teachers saying, "Thank you so much for such a simple but fun, creative idea. I can't wait to do this with my kids." When I hear feedback like that, I realize, *Wow, I'm making a difference.*

You can't be an extraordinary teacher on your own. Find a community of like-minded people, whether it's online or in your school community. Find people you can vent to and confide in, that you can ask questions of. No one is going to be amazing on their own. I think all those extraordinary teachers are the outcomes of extraordinary supporters and friends. Find your people.

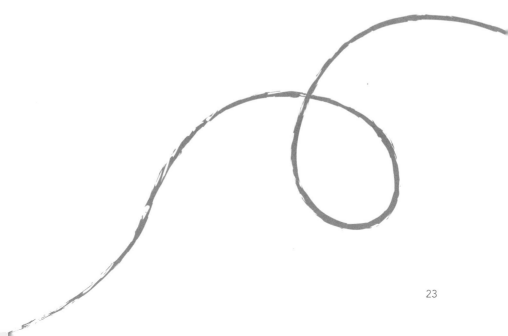

That Feeling of Fulfillment

Ms. Alexa Borota

NEW JERSEY

HIGH SCHOOL
ENGLISH

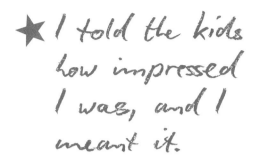
I told the kids how impressed I was, and I meant it.

I've kept a journal for as long as I could write. Sometimes, for fun, I love to go back and see that in third grade I would draw myself as a teacher. I've always wanted to be a teacher. As I grew older, I had a few other interests, but I always came back to teaching, specifically reading and writing. There was no other career path. I immediately went for education, and I knew that I wanted to teach high school.

I've always been a creative writer. When I was younger, I would write stories. I always have to have something to write in—I'm always writing down notes. If I hear a good quote, I have to write it down. I just have this intrinsic love of writing and reading. You get lost and renewed when you're reading.

It clicked for me in high school. I'd always loved to read, but then I started making connections between what we were learning in history and what we were reading in English. I realized I could read stories about what I learned in history. You might learn about the Salem witch trials in history, and then in English class, we'd read actual historical accounts and stories about it. I just thought it was cool, and I knew that that's what I wanted to teach.

I know this might sound cliché, but I put a lot of effort into (1) making learning fun and (2) trying to break it down. Yet each of those things comes with a problem: (1) life isn't always fun, and everything can't always be a game, and (2) what these students are expected to do, and what we have to teach, might require working on one assignment for a month straight because of how you have to break it down.

I teach Walt Whitman with Kanye West. Walt Whitman, in his time, was odd. He walked around naked with his friends. He was a weird guy to a lot of people. My students know a lot about Kanye West. Walt Whitman and Kanye aren't the same person, but my students can understand that Walt Whitman, to some degree, was a kind of "Kanye" of his time. It gets them interested. Little tricks like that break it down and make it fun. You take fiction and pair it with nonfiction. You take something old, and you pair it with new.

One of the reasons I chose to teach the novel *Long Way Down* by Jason Reynolds is that there are not a lot of words on each page. Students feel way less intimidated reading it, and then they have that feeling of fulfillment when they get through it. I pair it with a podcast that takes place in a high school in the South Side of Chicago, where there are a lot of issues, and many shootings and deaths. We read the novel, we listen to the podcast, and then we compare and do literary analysis.

Most teachers try to give their students a reason for writing. Sometimes it works, sometimes it doesn't. Some of my lessons have failed. But last year, I noticed that there was one particular skill that all my students were doing really well in—argumentative writing (ethos, pathos, logos). They were also really into *Long Way Down.* So I decided to trash the regular final exam I had lined up for them and instead I asked them to write a letter to Jason Reynolds, doing their best to persuade him to come to their graduation ceremony next year. They had to incorporate certain elements, like using interviews they'd watched and their book. And I told them there was a chance that we could actually send these to Jason Reynolds, to give them that purpose for writing. When I read their letters, I was blown away. I told the kids how impressed I was, and I meant it.

I sent the letters to Jason Reynolds's publishing company, and they forwarded them to him. On top of that, we made a TikTok to complement the letters and posted a video to our district's Instagram page. Jason Reynolds saw it and commented on it, and the next thing you know, I'm talking to his manager to set a date for him to come to our school and talk for Black History Month.

Someone needed to be onstage with him, but I wanted it to be facilitated by the students as much as possible. So, I pulled two students, and we practiced, developed questions, and set up the stage together. All the students who took part in the letter writing sat in the front rows of the auditorium. We had a packed house. The kids did such a good job interviewing him, and Jason Reynolds was so amazing. The students who took part in that, maybe even the ones who were just in the audience—I feel like they're going to remember that forever.

You Got This

Ms. Cara Smith

OREGON
HIGH SCHOOL MATH

I was one of those kids who, when I was little, my sisters and I would come home from elementary school, and we would play teacher with our chalkboard in the playroom. From an early age, I knew I liked math too.

As I got into high school, I was still thinking about teaching. A lot of people's perspectives on the career dissuaded me—they would say, "Teachers don't make a lot of money. It's a lot of hard work." I was getting a lot of negative feedback about the career, so for a little bit in high school, and then in early college, I wasn't sure teaching was the best idea for me. I started college never thinking about teaching at all. I went in as a genetics major until I realized I didn't really like genetics. I wanted to do something with math, so I changed my major and quickly realized nothing else in math sounded interesting except for teaching. So I went on to do a master's in education.

Math definitely has a stigma. There are so many negative stereotypes associated with it, but I am excited about it, and I want other people to be excited about it too. I start my class saying, "I know math's not everyone's favorite subject. I might not change you from being someone who hates math to be someone who loves math, but I'm hoping that the experience in this class will at least make you like it a little bit more."

★ Math definitely has a stigma . . . but I am excited about it, and I want other people to be excited about it too.

I don't see math as a lecture. I see it as more of a discussion about math. When I'm doing problems, I'll ask them, "Okay, what's my next step? What should I do?" And the kids will tell me what I'm supposed to do instead of me telling them. It's how I make sure they're engaged. Sometimes kids get scared to raise their hands and say something. I try to combat that earlier in the year by throwing candy to those who participate, trying to encourage them with that extrinsic motivation.

There are definitely kids who shut down when they don't get something. My job is navigating that and showing them that they can. Students sometimes have this ingrained belief that they're not good at math. I think sometimes it stems from parents who say things like, "I'm not good at math. You're probably not going to be good at math either." I'm trying to combat that on a daily basis. I have one student who comes into class every day and tells me, "It's not a math day for me." I say, "What are you talking about? You got this today. It's going to be good." I try to stay positive about it and show kids that they can do this, and tell them they're going to be okay until they believe it.

On the flip side, I had the privilege of being in charge of the Science, Technology, Engineering, and Mathematics (STEM) club this year. The kids who come to STEM club love math and just want to do more math in any way that they can. So there's a spectrum; you have the kids who don't like math and kids who are super excited about it.

There was one point in my first year where I was not at my best in the classroom and felt very frustrated and tired. When you're tired as a teacher, you have a short fuse and not as much patience as you normally would. My mentor teacher said, "I think you need to take a day." I felt so much better after having a day to center and take care of myself and then come back for the kids. I learned that every once in a while, if it's getting tough, take some time. The kids should have you when you're 100 percent.

I want to love what I do. As soon as I stop loving what I'm doing, I'm not going to do it anymore. If teaching gets to a point where it's too much or too overwhelming, I'm going to do what's best for me. My goal is not to become a crusty old teacher who hates her job. I want to be an amazing teacher who kids love, and I'm going to keep doing that until that's not me anymore.

The kids should have you when you're 100 percent.

Passionate People Make People Passionate

Mr. Nicholas Ferroni

NEW JERSEY

HIGH SCHOOL
HISTORY AND CULTURE STUDIES

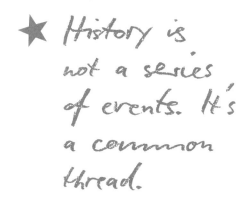

History is not a series of events. It's a common thread.

To be honest, I would be lying if I said I always wanted to be a teacher. I *have* always loved history. I thought it was the coolest subject in the world. I ended up doing my undergrad at Rutgers, where I played football and minored in art and majored in history. That's when I started to decide that maybe teaching was something I wanted to do as a full-time career. I've always had positive memories of the educators in my life. (Don't get me wrong, my family is great, and your mom *has* to love you.) It's the affirmation I got throughout my life from educators that left a profound impact on me and led me to be the person I am today. I've always wanted to help others in some form, and teaching history felt like the best of all the worlds.

I constantly have students walk in and say, "This is history. It happened. It's over. Who cares?" My challenge is to get them to invest in it. It's so hard to get kids to care about something. But passionate people make people passionate. That's why as educators we can't fake things that we're not passionate about. You have to love the subject area you teach because your students can tell when you don't.

Our history is about stories, and we leave out many. When I went to college and took African American studies and women's studies courses, I learned so much about the history of marginalized groups. It blew my mind, but also opened my mind to how there are facts and there's truth. I felt like for so much of my life, I'd been taught only one perspective of history while many different groups got left out. I decided that when I became a teacher, I was going to focus on making sure I shared all stories.

Also, in one of my college classes, I watched the brown-eyed/blue-eyed experiment by Jane Elliott in 1968, where she tries to teach her young white students about discrimination based on their eye color. I saw that and said, *When I'm a teacher, I'm going to try every way I can to not only do simulations and experiments but give my students the most powerful experience possible.* That led me to doing social experiments in my classroom with my students.

To me, stories and experience are the two best ways to teach history. I could teach you that the Declaration of Independence was signed on July 4, 1776. But I can also do an experiment where I have you sign a list of things you want to change about the school. Then I have my principal threaten you with punishment for insubordination if you keep your name on the list, and that helps me illustrate how that's a minor sacrifice. Will you take your name off? Now we can think about the Declaration of Independence in a new light. Signing it was treason. How far will you go for what you believe in? Pairing experiential simulation and engaging activities with the content allows my students to understand it before we even start.

I tend to teach history backward, by starting with something that's affecting their life now and tracing it back to what we're learning to show them how it's all connected—it also makes history very personal to them. History is not a series of events. It's a common thread. And we're all connected to it, whether or not we think we are.

Just as history is a form of making connections, it's important to me to connect with my fellow teachers. I share stories about teachers and teaching because I think stories move people more than information. If I say 57 percent of teachers don't make $60,000, people see that and think, *Oh, that sucks.* But if I tell them stories of teachers working a second job after their teaching day and still struggling—teachers who want to just teach, but they're forced to do other things so that they can't be the best teacher they can be—that punches at your gut a little bit more. No good person wants to see anyone else suffer, especially people who are making sacrifices to help other people's children. I try to bring awareness to lead to change. And I just like to celebrate, recognize, and let teachers know they're seen because so many feel like they're on an island.

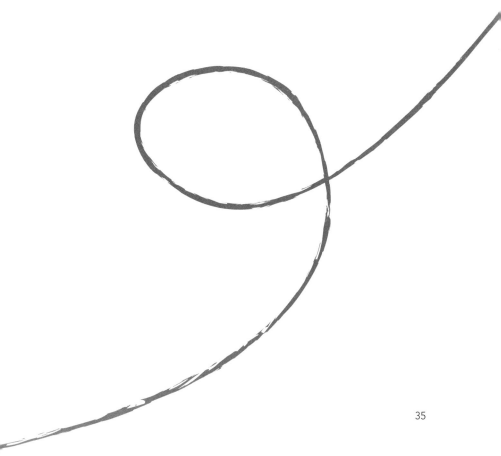

I think it's important that we teach the real stuff and that we don't sugarcoat things.
—ALEX LAHASKY

KIDS come to school to learn, but education isn't one-size-fits-all. Kindergarten teachers, for example, have a classroom full of kiddos merging together from different early experiences. Some students may have immigrated from another country and don't understand our language or culture. Some may not see themselves in our history because they are taught one perspective and not the others. Some may find utilizing technology and new ways of learning to be the only way they can grasp the content. History teachers have students who aren't interested in engaging with the material, and algebra teachers might combat math-phobia daily.

Yet every day, educators reach and teach children thanks to their creativity in lesson planning, their perpetual problem-solving, their passion for their subject matter, and their dedication to their kids.

They Educate

Changing the Game: Education in Action

Jaime Escalante *and* Making Math Memorable

Jaime Escalante taught in Bolivia for twelve years before coming to the United States. Once he arrived, he took on a variety of jobs while teaching himself English and then getting another degree.

The role he found himself in was as a high school math teacher in East Los Angeles. In an area challenged with poverty and gang violence, his school was threatened with losing its accreditation. But rather than leave, Escalante did something unexpected—he created an Advanced Placement (AP) calculus class. After he told his students that math would help them find good jobs, they got to work. That first year, eighteen of his students took the AP calculus exam and passed. As the years went on, more students passed the test and their performance gained national attention. Escalante's story was turned into the 1988 film *Stand and Deliver* and he was recognized by President Ronald Reagan, among others.

Nancie Atwell *and* Loving Literacy

Nancie Atwell took a job as a middle school teacher while trying to decide on a career as an English major. But teaching seventh and eighth graders, opening their eyes to new ideas, and watching them grow and mature became her passion. She realized, however, that the kids weren't passionate about reading and writing—and she set out to change that.

Instead of one assignment for every child, Atwell began to let the students choose what to read and write about. Engagement immediately increased. Eventually Nancie moved to Maine and opened the Center for Teaching and Learning, a development school. Students there read on average about forty books per year, far above national statistics, thanks to time set aside for solo reading in the classroom as well as homework of thirty minutes of reading at night. In 2015, Atwell won the Global Teacher Prize, an award of one million dollars presented to a teacher who has made an impact on the profession.

Howard Gardner *and* Multiple Intelligences

Traditional models of learning and intelligence suggest that there is one main form of intelligence that can be easily measured by simple tests such as the IQ test. But developmental psychologist Howard Gardner theorized that humans have many modes of processing information, and they can function independently from each other. In his theory of multiple intelligences, people have eight: spatial, logical-mathematical, bodily-kinesthetic, musical, linguistic, interpersonal, intrapersonal, and naturalist. Under this theory, a person has a mixture of intelligences and capabilities thanks to their unique mix of genetics and learning experiences.

For education, Gardner's theory suggests that students might learn best with personalized instruction. It also suggests that presenting a topic through multiple intelligence lenses can allow more students to understand it.

Gardner runs Harvard's Project Zero, a research program dedicated to learning, education, and tapping into all forms of human potential.

The Power of Education

Mr. Caleb Flores

COLORADO
HIGH SCHOOL ENGLISH LANGUAGE LEARNING

> *I know teaching English matters. It leads somewhere. I've seen it.*

In college, my roommate and I coached kids' football as a side thing, to try to help the community, and I found myself really happy going to practice and working with the fourth and fifth graders. I was originally a business major, but I quickly switched to education. To get my foot in the door as a teacher, I took a job in the school district working with the migrant education program. It's a grant-funded position nationwide, that works with students whose families are migrants and immigrants to the area. At the same time, I started working at the writing center at the local community college in their immigrant and refugee program.

I'm a Greeley, Colorado, native. My parents were also born here in Colorado, but their parents (my grandparents) all immigrated here from Mexico. So I was that second generation: I still appreciated and had a love for my culture, but my parents were first generation Latinos and shared with us some of the negative sides of that. Learning about the experiences of immigrants and English language learner students lit that fire underneath me and showed me this is what I'm supposed to do with my life. I look back on those years and I'm just so grateful for those experiences.

I know the power of education; I've seen it change lives within my own family. I think all students are capable, and I think all students can show up and work and put in their best effort. But there is just something different about a student from somewhere else. They've seen hardships and they had struggles that we sometimes can't relate to. For them to be sitting at a desk with me and to have the utmost respect and eagerness about being in a classroom—that really excited me. I thought, *These guys are just excited to be here.* I know that by them going to school, it's going to change the trajectory of their future and their family's future.

I have students who are brand new to the country. We mostly get Spanish-speaking immigrant and refugee students from Mexico and Central America. Recently, we had an influx of students from Venezuela and Colombia. Over the past ten years, in Greeley, we've had students from East Africa—Somalia and Eritrea—and Southeast Asia—Myanmar and Thailand and other areas. In addition to languages, there are cultural differences. For example, some of the students from Southeast Asia were living in a civil war, and we had students migrating here from both sides. They were told, when they were young, not to associate with people from the opposing side, so getting them in a classroom together took a lot of conversation and healing. Of course, students are resilient, and they eventually became friends.

Education-wise, our students are really all over the place. Some have gone to school. Some have been in refugee camps for the past several years and have had no schooling. Ours can't be a one-size-fits-all approach. I'm the teacher who shows up to their first meeting, and we have a conversation. "Who are you? Where are you from? And what are your goals for being here?" We try to personalize that plan and their education. We tell our students, "We believe in the power of education and access to it, and we're going to do whatever we can as a school to get you to your goals." In my class, Language Development One, we start with "Hello," and and we move forward. I really try to make language learning fun, but mostly it's about fostering a community of acceptance and of trial and failure and eventually learning.

My second or third year at Greeley West, a new student enrolled from Myanmar. He was brand new to English and he was still very much learning. (In his first presentation, he used lyrics from the song "Smack That" by Akon.) Over the years, he started to grow, and I really saw his language improve. It's been years since he graduated, but a few months ago, I was at one of the local Asian markets when I noticed a nice car pull up. That student got out of the car with his brother. We got to catch up, and he told me he was working at one of the meatpacking plants outside of the city. He said that because his English was so good and because of the leadership skills he showed at work, he got promoted. He's the shift supervisor, and he said he's making more money than he ever believed he could.

I told my wife afterward that out of what we did in class, not all of it was probably relevant to that position, but I know teaching English matters. It leads somewhere. I've seen it: the kids who are the first in their families to graduate high school, English language learners who get good jobs, and the students who even go on to college. It just makes it all the more rewarding to see that it does work. Even on the hard days, we're doing this for a reason.

Leveling the Playing Field

Mr. Shane Baker

KENTUCKY
THIRD GRADE GENERAL EDUCATION

A couple of years ago, I joined the inaugural group of edtech (Educational Technology) ambassadors in our school system. The group got to learn about and use different types of technology for the classroom, like 3D printing, robotics, and other apps. My favorite one was the green screen kit. I use that for literacy and to encourage my kids with a new publication opportunity instead of just typing what they write or making slides. I had a lower group of readers and writers in my class this year, and their main worry was, "Do I have to write everything?" I could tell them no, that we just needed a basic script. Using the green screen helped them a lot and played to their strengths.

It's fun to see how technology levels the playing field for some of our kids—those who have struggled to catch back up after the pandemic or English language learners, for example. My school fluctuates around the 50 percent mark for English learners. I think for Kentucky, especially, we have a very diverse school. Our students represent over at least thirty different countries that I can think of.

Technology can help us find and use programs that give them more voice in what they're trying to say. The fact that almost every web program out there has some sort of voice-to-text feature is great for our kids. You can see when they start to get it, when they grab a knack for it, and how they

★ *Education is a tool that can help remedy a lot of our social ills.*

want to keep doing it. I had one kid who was so happy with being able to speak and record and then use the software to cut out all those little parts where he paused. Sometimes you have time to indulge them, and sometimes you don't. Sometimes, they even figure it out faster than me.

Through edtech conferences and opportunities, I've learned a lot and have been able to talk with other people who also understand technologies and shoot ideas around with them. We try to figure out how we can use it not to just use it, but to build upon whatever standards or content we're already teaching and give kids a real-world, applicable tool. I try to make connections and make them mean something. I never try to throw in technology just because.

But on the flip side, I do see that education is rapidly evolving, especially with the release of AI to the public. Some people are very resistant to it and others embrace it (maybe a little too much). But I think there can be a good balance between the two. I try to find that balance because I want to teach kids how to use technology, but I don't want it to be the end-all, be-all.

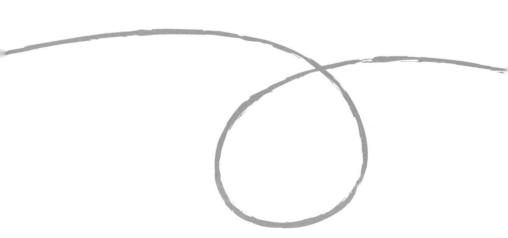

I think as teachers part of our responsibility is to teach students not just how to use technology, but why and when to use it. The problems come when they're not given explicit instructions. We're not teaching the social components like digital citizenship and how to be responsible with it. I don't have the perfect solution for that yet. I'm trying my best to integrate technology while also setting boundaries.

I do think that education is a tool that can help remedy a lot of our social ills. I wanted to be part of that, and I figured elementary would be a great place to start, especially with the staggering lack of male educators in this age group. I love my job. I love what I do. I'm in it for the kids, watching them grow and be able to change, and to hopefully craft a better world.

My best advice for new teachers is you've got to be your own kind of teacher. Especially in my first few years, I would see what someone else was doing and feel like I wasn't doing enough. It's healthy, to a certain extent, to challenge oneself. But I think my kids have grown more because I am who my students need at this moment in time, whether they realize it or not. If you try to be someone else, you're just going to fail.

The Ones Who Come Back

Ms. Kirsten Irwin

MICHIGAN

THIRD GRADE
GENERAL EDUCATION

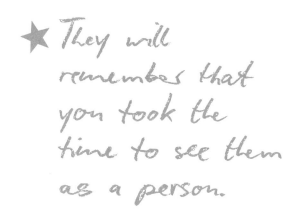
They will remember that you took the time to see them as a person.

I had an amazing second grade teacher who really inspired me. Years later, as an adult, I got to talk with her again and tell her, "You're the reason."

My first year of teaching, the class just meshed with me; they meshed with each other. It really spoiled me. Your first year is typically not your best year—you're working on classroom management; you're figuring things out—but this class was the epitome of a classroom family.

Something I am very passionate about is that college students should be in the classroom the minute they become an education major, if not before. I had quite a few friends in college who were in education. Two and a half years went by, and the first time they stepped into a classroom they realized, "This is not for me. I can't do this every day." They ended up leaving, or they finished their degree and didn't love teaching. You have to love teaching. It's not a career you can just float by in.

My mentor for third grade was an awesome woman. But my mentor for preschool was a saint. She'd been doing it for I don't know how many years and she just flawlessly and effortlessly had classroom management and classroom relationships. She made it a point to learn the new things in education that were coming up, making sure she was up to date on how kids were changing and how education was changing. From her my biggest lesson was that teaching has to be flexible. (I have a coworker who says her favorite F word is *flexible*. And you know you'll have three students in a third grade class who get the joke.)

Third grade just kind of landed in my lap, and I love it. The best way to describe it is the kids still very, very much love their teacher, but they have some independence. And the ones that don't, you can teach, right? It's an age where there's lots of growth. They're still cute. They're still sweet to their teacher. They're not too cool for school (most of them). They have crushes—I have a box full of notes to prove it—but they don't really date yet. Some of them get sarcasm and some of them don't. So that's really fun.

If you get excited about what you're teaching, the kids will be excited. It doesn't matter what the material is. I don't love fractions, but I act like fractions are the coolest thing you will ever learn in math, because I know it's going to be hard for kids in third grade. I made up Fraction Land. Here, we do movement activities, fraction flowers, and turn their names into a fraction. Anytime we start math, I say, "Get your Fraction Land hats on!" I sing and dance for them. If you can sing it to them or feed it to them, they'll remember it forever.

I think extraordinary teachers have relationships with their students, and I think that that comes first, above and beyond anything else. You have to see students as people and not just students. Our job as teachers is to make them better people. Yes, we have content to teach, and hopefully, you can get the content across. But the kids are not going to care about the content if they don't think you care about them.

If you would like to become an extraordinary teacher, you need to build relationships with your students. That's harder to do with some students than others—some students don't want a relationship. There's a quote out there that says something along the lines of, some students are at school to learn, and some students are at school to have a safe place, to be loved, to be cared for, to get a meal. Kids have different reasons for going to school. Of course, the easiest kids to build a relationship with, and to teach, are the ones who are there to learn and who have all their needs met at home and an involved family helping them. Your hardest kids to teach, the hardest ones to build a relationship with, are going to be those kids, those students, those people who are not getting their needs met at home. It matters that you value them as a person. They're going to remember that for the rest of their life. Who cares if they remember long division? But they will remember that you took the time to see them as a person. And those are going to be the ones who come back and make you cry when they tell you how much you mattered to them. They're the ones who are sitting in an interview in fifteen years saying, "I remember my second grade teacher."

Room for Them to Be Excited

Ms. Lindsey Jacobson

IDAHO

MIDDLE SCHOOL
LIFE SCIENCES

I'm early in my career, and definitely still learning. It's not until you're actually in class that you learn how to teach and be a teacher. But it's such a special job to have. Every day I'll walk around my classroom and think, *Is this really my job? I get paid to do this?*

I never wanted to teach middle school—middle school sounded awful. It wasn't until I did my student teaching that I found I loved middle schoolers. I had so much fun with them. They're definitely a handful, and behavior issues are a lot worse. But they still get excited about school, and they want to impress you. If I say, "Today we're doing this and it's going to be super fun," they get on board with it very fast.

With middle schoolers, there can be behavior issues and disrespect, which can be hard for teachers to deal with. I would encourage anyone experiencing that to think, *Okay, clearly something in this kid's life is not going right, and maybe they need you now more than ever.* They need a strong, competent teacher, because they clearly don't have a figure like that at home if they're showing disrespect at school. You can teach these kids how to not be disrespectful and be the change for them. Instead of having this mindset of feeling underappreciated and disrespected, I see it as having a really powerful role in the lives of kids.

Okay, clearly something in this kid's life is not going right, and maybe they need you now more than ever.

Here's my classroom management tip: Go into teaching middle school knowing that middle school boys and girls are going to act like middle school boys and girls. You can't expect them to make smart decisions all the time. They're going to complain. They're going to talk when they're not supposed to. You're going to face all of these issues because they're twelve and they're still developing and they're going through all these changes. You have to have that understanding or you're going to go crazy.

I think science is the most fun subject to teach, just because you can do so much hands-on learning. Science is all around you. You can apply it. You can say, "Have you ever wondered why this happens?" and then show students how it works and help them understand the world around them. A lesson that could be just taking notes on a boring lecture can become an opportunity to go outside and find a certain specimen. We can have a lot of fun with it. Putting those two together—the middle schoolers who still get excited about learning and science that is all around us—we can do so much with it.

My favorite thing to teach is genetics. We learn about DNA and then we go into genetics and heredity. It's just so fun for them, because they can ask, "My parents have this trait—is that why I look the way I do?" We can actually see when we make Punnett squares why it's not a surprise that a trait expresses itself. It can be a little bit awkward because we have to talk about how life is made, so that's always fun to navigate. But they can begin to understand why three siblings who all came from the same parents look similar but different. It's fun to see the aha moments.

They're at an age where they want to understand the things around them—they can see plants grow, but they don't know *how* plants grow or *how* they make energy. They don't know how *humans* make energy. They obviously know we have to eat food and we have to breathe, but to actually understand what happens in our body when we eat food and when we breathe oxygen, we can make cellular respiration and healthy versus unhealthy food applicable for them.

Maybe for some kids, my class will inspire them to want to be a scientist one day. But I feel like I have a special opportunity to teach them life skills and push them to grow into who they're meant to be. Finding a way for them to come into my class and be excited and ready to learn, ready to grow, ready to make friendships—I found that is almost more important at this grade level. I'm not as worried about them remembering every science concept that I teach. Obviously, that's still important. But if they can come into my class not being super confident and leave feeling confident in themselves, I feel like that's more special.

I'm living my dream of being a teacher; I think it's the best job ever. I encourage anyone to look into it if they want a very rewarding career. At the start of this school year, I started posting on social media about all kinds of things about teaching. It's been really cool to see it grow into what it has. People comment, "This makes me so excited to be a teacher," and I'm so grateful for that. I feel like there is a lot of negativity around the profession, and I'm glad that I get to have a page where I can show people that teaching actually can be really cool and fun and exciting—and that you can be a teacher who also has a life outside of teaching. Maybe valuing teachers is also about seeing that teachers have lives, showing the actual breadth of it.

Teaching Kids How to Think

Mr. Alex Lahasky

KANSAS

HIGH SCHOOL
HISTORY

History allows us the opportunity to develop empathy.

I teach American history, and some of the most memorable teachers that I had in high school and professors that I had in college were my history professors. Their knowledge often crossed over into wisdom, and their ability to command a room and tell a story was probably the real inspiration for me to get into this profession. One of the things that makes a good teacher is a real passion for their discipline and a belief that their discipline matters.

History doesn't teach kids what to think; it teaches kids *how* to think. It teaches kids how to deal with complexity and nuance, because we don't live in a world that's black and white—it's overwhelmed by shades of gray.

Let's use the example of Abraham Lincoln—and if any of my students read this book, they will roll their eyes at my mention of Lincoln because I talk about him all the time. It's not because Lincoln was this flawless, mythical figure in American history. In fact, it's the opposite. He was complex and paradoxical and even contradictory at times, but studying Lincoln allows us to see a really difficult problem and how a capable but imperfect human being tried to address that problem. The skill of grappling with that complexity is one of the things that I think makes history really important.

Teaching history today is different than it has been in years or decades. It's an age-old adage in my line of work that history is critical for the survival of democracy, but there's another aspect of historical education that I don't think gets enough credit that I'm, in particular, pretty passionate about. It is that history can also develop virtues and social-emotional skills that we appear to be increasingly lacking.

There's lots of research that suggests we're having a harder time understanding one another; political polarization is increasing, and people are less likely to have good friends who vote for a different political party than they do. I submit that a sound history education is perhaps a remedy for that. History allows us the opportunity to develop empathy.

At the beginning of every school year, I tell my students that we're not just learning dates, names, and facts. We're making evaluations, judgments, and arguments that are based on the evidence that we can pull together, and that gives us power. None of these historical figures are here to defend themselves. But by taking on their perspectives and considering their circumstances—circumstances that are not our own—we can better evaluate them. I would argue that developing that skill and habit of mind allows us to hopefully, in turn, better understand the people we interact with on a daily basis.

Something I hear a lot when I talk to people outside of the profession, in particular outside of the discipline, is, "I wouldn't want to touch such-and-such topic with a ten-foot pole. I wouldn't want to touch slavery or racism or economic inequality at all. How do you tiptoe around that?" The answer is I don't.

We learn about immigration during the Gilded Age, when millions of immigrants were coming to the United States from Eastern and Southern Europe. Their culture was different than that of most Americans who were already here, and these new immigrants faced hardships as a result of that. In my view, if a student today can learn to empathize with a late-nineteenth-century first-generation immigrant, hopefully they'll also be able to empathize with a classmate who is a first-generation immigrant or who has a background that is different than their own.

I think it's important that we teach the real stuff and that we don't sugarcoat things. That we allow students space to grapple with the good and the bad and then make their own conclusions and evaluations from it. That's a precedent that I try to set early in the school year: "We're going to talk about some hard things, and some of these topics are going to affect you and your classmates differently."

I'm blessed to work in a school that has some great students. They have an understanding from the beginning of the year that some days, when we come into this class, it'll be fun and light, and other days it's going to be heavy, and the conversations are going to be hard. I have to commend the students for their willingness to get their hands dirty when those topics come up and to approach them in a way that's academically responsible and respectful of their peers who have different ideas. Our conversations in the classroom are hopefully the building blocks for a young adult who is going to have that same respect and empathy for others when they leave my classroom.

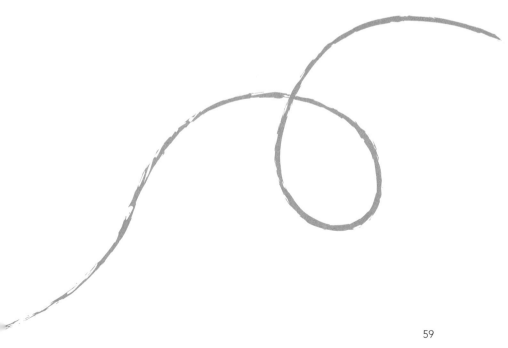

We can catch kids who some others can't.

— MICHELLE BOUCHER SMITH

THROUGH everyday challenges of students'

behavior, administration issues, endless paperwork—and through unprecedented challenges to the profession like staffing shortages—and more, teachers somehow keep teaching. With everything facing educators, what keeps them showing up every day? It boils down to their why, which is often their students—and their unwavering belief in trying to make a difference. They persist against the odds, and in doing so, they uncover breathtaking moments of connection, of reward, of humanity.

They Connect

Changing the Game: Making Connections

Marva Collins *and* Creating Her Own School

After working in the Chicago Public School system for over a decade, Marva Collins decided she was tired of what she saw as the neglect of inner-city students. To do better for her children and local kids, she created the Daniel Hale Williams Westside Preparatory School, which operated out of the second floor of her home. Starting with just four students, soon her class sizes grew and included kids who public schools were sure could never be taught. But Collins found a way and her students scored higher than their grade level on standardized tests. Collins's story was featured in national news media, such as *Good Morning America* and *Newsweek*.

Collins returned to Chicago public schools in 1996 and continued to improve school ratings and trained more than one hundred thousand teachers before her death in 2015.

John Goodlad *and* Changing How Schools Teach

John Goodlad conducted an eight-year study that took place in thirty-eight schools, tracking students from kindergarten through their senior year in high school. The findings, which were published in 1983, showed the disconnect between students, teachers, and the subject matter, and worse yet, how poorly schools prepared kids to be citizens in the real world.

Throughout his career, including time as a professor at the University of Washington and as dean at the Graduate School for Education at UCLA, Goodlad put forward new ideas for changing education, including doing away with grade levels, improving early learning, and changing how teachers are trained. At the University of Washington, he formed the Center for Educational Renewal, and after he retired, he founded the Institute for Educational Inquiry. Goodlad believed that Congressional bills and educational policy were all well and good, but at the end of the day, each school has immense power in shaping the education system.

Edmund Gordon *and* Closing the Achievement Gap

Psychologist and scholar Edmund Gordon grew up in the 1920s in segregated Goldsboro, North Carolina. He was sure he would go to college, and he did. But he struggled at Howard University and was suspended for a semester for falling behind in his work. He continued to struggle while pursuing a graduate degree in psychology in New York City. Discussing these experiences with his friend and mentor W. E. B. Du Bois, Gordon started to think about why certain people succeed and others don't.

Gordon went on to study the achievement gap—the differences in student achievement when those students are grouped by, for example, race or socioeconomic status. His ideas that underprivileged and minority students' negative experiences could affect their education lead to his many accolades. In 1956, President Lyndon B. Johnson commissioned Gordon to design the Head Start Program to provide early childhood education to families in need. Today, the program serves nearly one million children.

Finding That Turning Point

Ms. Alexis Arias

CALIFORNIA

ALTERNATIVE ED
ENGLISH AND SENIOR STUDIES

I have to get them to buy into themselves.

I teach in alternative education. At our site, that means we provide students the opportunity to re-earn and retain credits they missed out on in their original school during their freshmen and sophomore years. We offer different timelines. Sure, we don't have things like AP classes, nor do we have many elective opportunities, but some of our students find that they just need the focus, the time, and the elimination of distractions that a traditional school has. We can provide those things.

The challenge that I face, and many at our school face, is getting through to our students what they need to earn and learn to fill in the gaps. At the same time, we have to have a lot of social-emotional awareness for what they've experienced or what got them here. It can be a challenge knowing their past and not judging them for it yet still pushing them to do more and be more for themselves.

I've had kids say, "You think this is bad? You didn't see me my freshman and sophomore years!" I have to say, "That's great. But you've done 70 percent of the credit, and I see that you can do 80 or 90 percent. You can earn more." I have to get them to buy into themselves and buy into a process of doing even more while at the same time giving them validation for the growth that they've had. Pushing them to the next level can be a challenge.

Some people have hesitations about coming to work at a school site like ours. Historically, it's had a bad reputation for troubled kids, rebellious and criminalized kids. But people don't understand until they're here in the classroom how wrong that reputation is. Back at the traditional schools, I've had more kids upset and frustrated with me and not listen to me; I've had more disruptions there. The kids really want to be here versus the kids who are forced to be there; in traditional schools, the kids often aren't mature enough. People really underestimate how much these factors benefit the students and me as their teacher.

I experienced the Las Vegas shooting in 2017. One of my immediate reflections was that the most traumatic thing that's ever happened to me occurred when I was thirty-three—well into adulthood, when my mind was more mature. I had the ability to rationalize, cope, and deal with everything afterward. I had support systems all around me; I had so much going for me at that point in my life. I quickly made the connection that my students who experience similar traumas are not afforded all of these advantages. Often, they don't have support systems, or their networks are smaller. I remember thinking right away, *I am lucky that at thirty-three I have to live through this. I get to work through this in my mind and in my heart with all that I have going for me.* My kids aren't always as fortunate.

When I was in the hospital, I was able to advocate for myself. I was using my words to vocalize and to communicate what hurt me, what pained me, what I thought I needed. When I was at home in recovery, I had the confidence to say to people, "I need you to let me go back to work. I need you to let me start driving. Not doing these things is holding me back from moving on. You are holding me in this freeze, and I mentally and emotionally need to go back to who I was. I need to go back to being teacher, mom, coach. I need to go back to these things to feel like I'm getting my life back."

My realization was that our students don't have those capabilities. Not all students have that self-advocacy, that ability to communicate and to use the right words for how they feel and what they need. They may not have had that modeled for them. They may have tried, and it was shut down; it wasn't listened to, it wasn't validated, whatever the case may be. My communicating and self-advocating was something I recognized helped me in my process. Our students, on the other hand, who have gone through their own traumas at younger points in their lives, have not yet gained the ability to do that.

There's a famous teacher saying, "It's not happening to me, it's not happening at me, but it's happening in front of me." I don't know where in the real world we think we can automatically be served our expectation right away. If we think that way, we're going to be walking around in life very unhappy. But I've found a turning point with too many kids to give up. That's what I have to hold on to. That's what I have to use as encouragement to keep going.

It's not happening to me, it's not happening at me, but it's happening in front of me.

Because They Want to Be a Part of It

Ms. Michelle Boucher Smith

KANSAS

ELEMENTARY SCHOOL
MUSIC

I did not go into music education immediately. I took general education classes, and then through that, I went into music therapy. Then I observed a friend in an elementary school music class. She was magic in the classroom. That's all it took. It was love at first sight. The connection she had with her students, the fun activities they did—the class brought me back to times when I had music and I thought, *I want to re-create that for my own classroom.* I thought if I can bring that much joy to a kid, just one kid, I'm sold.

In our district, we're a military site, and we also have a federal penitentiary. Both mean that we have kiddos coming and going. We live in a time where so many kids come from families that don't trust teachers, so building that trust with kids is huge. You need to let them know, number one, you love them. But, number two, you're going to hold them accountable. And if you don't have those things, those relationships will never work.

A big part of building that trust is understanding where they come from, because my upbringing will not be the same as what those I'm teaching are experiencing. I've had to really change how I see them in my classroom and realize that music may not be the most important thing on their mind at that minute.

I thought if I can bring that much joy to a kid, just one kid, I'm sold.

I've always thought about going back to college and kind of revamping how teachers are taught to design lesson plans and handle class management because they're currently not getting what they need. I think teachers are coming out of college thinking, "I can't wait to decorate my classroom. I'm going to have this rule and this rule and they're all going to come in and sit down." But we don't live in that society anymore. Kids are throwing chairs, screaming, throwing fits; they are throwing instruments.

It's hard for me to see so many teachers, right now especially, leave the profession because of what they end up dealing with—and I know what they're dealing with, because I went through it. Teachers aren't taught how to handle the behaviors they encounter, and that's not just in the state of Kansas or Arizona. It's all over. I think a lot of people think teachers are being overdramatic about what they see and experience at school, but it's real.

I almost quit teaching because the behaviors were so unbelievable. They were so atrocious, and I thought, *I'm not a good teacher. I can't even get these kids to sit down where they're supposed to.* Thank God for my mom. I would call her every day crying. But it's not in me to quit, and I would constantly go back over every moment: What didn't work? What can I try again? And I would continue to do that every single day.

I revamped how I taught everything, including my classroom management. Now I help other teachers handle behaviors and build those relationships with their students. Even if I'm on my plan time, I go get those kids in distress and we talk. We go through those behavior strategies: "You can be okay even though you're upset. You can be mad, but you still have to follow expectations."

Even to this day, after teaching twenty-four years, it's still a learning curve. I'm still trying to find out what's going to work with each kid. I've mentored two different teachers this year alone, trying to help them understand that you may not be able to teach your entire lesson plan—you may not even get through a third of it. A majority of your time is spent building those relationships. Because if you don't have that, you won't ever teach anything.

I do musicals with every grade. My first year in the district, I thought it would be impossible, but we got it done and they loved it. The kids got to see their family, their people, their humans out in the audience excited for them, and they ate it up. The amount of people who come to our programs is mind-blowing. Everybody in the family comes. We can't put enough chairs out. Once the kids see that, they ask, "When are we going to do another musical?" This is coming from kids who didn't want to do it in the first place.

People ask, "Why would you do one for every grade?" Because they need it. They need to see that love and support from their families.

At the same time, I had a second grader who hadn't made it through any of the rehearsals because of his behavior. But he showed up the night of the performance—he actually walked there, with his older cousin, who's in fourth grade, and his sister. He showed up so they could come to their musical too. Oh, it makes me tear up every time I think about it because that was important to him.

I told him I was so super proud of him for doing that. Granted, he was back to his shenanigans the next day and causing a ruckus, God love him. But for him to know that I was proud of him that he made that choice—it's those moments in teaching where you realize this is why you do it. I do it because they want to be there. They want to be a part of it.

We can reach kids through PE, art, STEM, library, and music that maybe the classroom teacher can't, and that's why I'm such a huge proponent for all of these specials and electives. We can catch kids who some others can't.

Ready for the World

Mr. Brandon Peña

TEXAS
HIGH SCHOOL ENGLISH

★ *I have the ability to impact students who need somebody to be a positive person in their life.*

Being a teacher is definitely not for the faint of heart. It's kind of like you're going into battle every day and just hoping for the best. Sometimes you don't even know what that battle is. Maybe this kid is going to ask me for the fifteenth time to go to the restroom, or they're going to pull out their phone even though they know the rules. Then there's the hormones of it all. One minute, they're happy and laughing, and two seconds later they're crying in the corner because their best friend just said something off the wall to them—and then they're mad at you, and you weren't even involved.

For me, it's figuring out how to harness all of that and still help them grow as a person. That's what I always tell my kids: "I want you to know the content. I want you to know reading. I want you to know writing. But I also need you to learn certain skills for beyond high school, beyond college; I want you to be ready for the real world." Now is a great time for us to start going over these things.

I always try to lead with patience. You're going to have days when students will just put their heads down. They are not interested. My superpower of sorts is that I can be patient when it comes to kids and their range of emotions. I got it from my grandma. We're very compassionate people. I try to see all perspectives.

That is also what makes teaching hard in general, because you're not just a teacher. I'm not just presenting content and grading assignments. I wear a lot of hats. Sometimes you're the counselor, sometimes you're the nurse, sometimes you're the lawyer, the judge. There are so many things that you are, and it can be exhausting.

It comes down to the question: *Why am I doing this?* People ask, "What's your why?" Your why can change day to day, minute to minute. Sometimes my why is having to get through this lesson. Sometimes it's that student in the corner who's not speaking up for themselves. This year I had a student ask me to go to their choir concert, so I did. When I saw him, I asked where his family was. He told me they didn't really believe in school, so they didn't come. I cried in the back of the room. My why is to be here for him and for other students like that.

I'm proud of you because you show up every day, because you try.

There was another student—I didn't have him in class—who was considered the bad kid on campus, a kid who was always in trouble. When I did morning duty, every now and then I would say to him, "Hey, how's it going?" or, "How was your football game?" He started to engage with me, and that turned in to daily check-ins. He was one of those kids who had a really rough background, a really rough home life. At the end of the school year, I told him, "I want you to know I'm proud of you." He asked, "Proud of me for what?" I told him, "I'm proud of you because you show up every day, because you try. It doesn't matter what any other adults or students tell you; you can do anything you want to in your life. You are capable of doing great things." He just looked at me and then went back to his friends. At dismissal on the last day of school, he came up to me and bumped me. It wasn't a handshake or a hug, but he gave me a little bump; it was a sign of respect. That's my why. It's not because I teach writing, which I love; it's not because I teach reading, which I love. It's because I have the ability to impact students who need somebody to be a positive person in their life.

You're not going to be every student's favorite teacher, and that's okay, as long as they have somebody. That's why school matters. Sometimes it's the safest place for kids. It's the place where they can just be and not have all the extra worries of day-to-day life. You can't always fix it. You can't fix their home life. You can't fix a lot of things. But what you can do is give them kindness, give them grace, and give them a space and opportunity to just be themselves.

Taking the Time to Check Up on People

Ms. Khadesia Latimer

SOUTH CAROLINA

ELEMENTARY SCHOOL ART

My class is about culture and empathy and the real world.

Art was my thing in school. I didn't do sports, because I can barely walk in a straight line to be honest. But art was always something that I looked forward to every single year that I was in school. That's what led me to teaching art: the passion for the kids and the passion to create art with children.

Kids think about things a lot differently than adults do. Sometimes they take things very literally and sometimes they can go off into left field and come up with something way different than you wanted them to do. But that's part of art, right? You get to decide what you want it to be regardless of my directions. I always try to make sure that my projects aren't cookie cutter. We may all start off with the same idea, but my favorite thing, when I pick up all the papers at the end of class, is that they're all different in some type of way.

When I first got into education, I was discouraged because teachers would drop their kids off to my class like I was the babysitter. They had the important job. But in my class, we're not making crafts, and we're not making little things to take home and hang on a Christmas tree. My class is about culture and empathy and the real world. I think sometimes art teachers begin to feel like they're only there to hold the kids over until it's time for them to go back to their other classes. But it's not true at all. If we weren't there, the school would be a totally different place.

The students I teach only see me once a week, so when they do see me, I feel like I'm a celebrity. There is less stress when it comes to my class and my content. When they come in, they don't have to worry about, "I haven't met this goal," or, "I haven't done this," or, "I didn't do my homework." I always tell them, "Hey, come here and do what you can do. That's all I'm asking you to do."

I feel like the kids decompress when they come in my room. I always teach first, and then after we pass everything out, we work silently for five minutes. We use those five minutes to start that creative process without any distractions. I have some kids ask, before we even start, "Are we doing silent art today?" They're almost saying, "I really need these five minutes." It's a great way to start off the class and get everybody in that creative mode. Once they've had those five minutes, I let them talk and it just all flows. You can see they have a weight lifted off their shoulders.

I do have some kids who come in and say, "Ms. Latimer, I'm just not good at art," "So-and-so's artwork looks better than mine," or, "I can't do that." Whenever I hear that bad self-talk, I tell them that negativity is like bad germs: We do not want them, and we don't want to share your bad germs with others because then that can make them sick. Negativity is the same. You might not like what you're working on. That's totally fine. Ms. Latimer has done plenty of projects that she did not like and that's okay. That's part of the process sometimes.

The conversation about mental health in schools is surfacing more and we're doing a better job of recognizing it. Mental health issues also affect younger kids. It's important to have those conversations. In my class, it can be just taking the time to teach empathy. Or if a student's having a bad day, to say, "Hey, would it help if we stepped outside to talk, and then maybe I can figure out how to help you?"

Even though class can get very hectic and busy, we need to recognize the atmosphere in the room. We can't forget to scan the room and see if everybody's okay. Every class, during those five minutes of silent art, I take the time to notice whose head is down. Do they need to take a nap or do they need to go talk to somebody? I've learned over the years the importance of just taking the time to check up on people, even if it's just for a second. Even if they don't want to talk to me, maybe I can find somebody for them to talk to.

Negativity is like bad germs: We do not want them, and we don't want to share your bad germs with others . . .

Building Empathy

Mr. John Rodney

As I grew up during elementary, middle, and high school, I developed a love for English and a strong bond with my English teachers. I said to myself, "I want to be *that* teacher who is *that* figure in a student's life." For me, my parents could only support me so much. When it came to developing my reading and writing abilities and my creative senses, my English teachers were the people I gravitated toward. So, teaching English was a natural pathway for me to take.

I'm an openly LGBTQ+ educator. Especially in high school, when I was dealing with identity, teachers provided safe spaces for me. Teachers recognized something I hadn't yet understood about myself, they gave me space for self-realization, and they basically said, "I see you and it's okay." I didn't even really recognize what they did for me until much later in life.

★ I've seen students read a story that makes their hearts burst open a little bit and, in turn, makes their worlds bigger.

I teach middle school. You would think that by middle school students understand how they're supposed to act. But we're finding that's not the case, especially with what they're consuming through technology. What kids find entertaining are not necessarily the most empathetic acts. Take, for example, viral prank videos, which essentially say that making people laugh is worth someone's terror.

Some of the people who create content online don't always have the best intentions for young people at heart, yet young people are consuming so much of that content. In school, we have to take the time to say, "Acting like this is not normal," or if it is normal, it's not acceptable. It's not honorable. In order for kids to understand what's okay and not okay, we need them to see and understand the humanity in others. We have to really drive home these ideas of *What does an empathetic person look like? What are the correct actions of empathetic people?*

When we're focusing on academic skills but we're not building empathy, we're missing a bigger opportunity. Stories give us a way. Teach the skills, yes, but let's use a quality piece of writing that can also layer on a piece of empathy. You can build in representative stories effortlessly. And the lessons don't have to be about the stories themselves. We can use any story to compare characters—how is a character in one story like a character in another story? How are they different? What are the plotlines? The story is a tool and character traits can be normalized—girls can be strong; boys can feel more than just anger.

Stories are constantly evolving, so it's about finding the one that's at the right grade level and that's going to really touch hearts. My favorite story will always be one that lets them empathize with the character, and that's going to get them thinking. I've seen students read a story that makes their hearts burst open a little bit and, in turn, makes their worlds bigger.

I used to teach high school, and I appreciated so much how seniors would come back and tell me how I helped them academically. I did feel validated by that. But with middle schoolers, you definitely feel like you're getting through and getting them to think. If you get them thinking for a moment, then you know that a thread has been left for them, and it might change the trajectory of some part of their lives.

I feel I sleep better at night when I know I did everything I could.
— DIEGO NAPOLES

YES, teachers offer academic support by tailoring instruction to make sure every child has the assistance they need to navigate the content at hand. But often, life from outside the school walls find its way in, and a teacher's support extends beyond classroom matters. Gently being there for a fourth grader processing family issues, supporting a student struggling to read, helping a middle school girl navigate the complexity of her emotions, or finding a way to get through to a disconnected high school senior— these things might not be written into the job description, but extraordinary teachers go beyond what's expected of them every day for their students. Driven by compassion, humanity, and love, they reach out to, connect with, and see kids for who they truly are—and help them through.

They Support

Changing the Game: Supporting Students

Elaine Schwartz *and the* Center School

Elaine Schwartz was born in New Jersey, and, after getting a theater degree from the University of Illinois, she married and moved to New York City. She worked as a teacher and a counselor for years before teaching at Fordham's Graduate School of Education.

Later, she founded the Center School in 1982 in New York City and designed it to be different. The school offered classes to students of multiple grade levels. They invited the students to parent-teacher conferences and gave them narrative report cards rather than As, Bs, Cs, and Ds. Students were also required to participate in theater to help them gain confidence, something Schwartz believed in deeply. Schwartz became principal of the Center School and stayed there until her retirement over forty years later.

Shirley Hufstedler *and the* First DOE

Shirley Hufstedler was among the first women to graduate from Stanford Law School and practiced law for several years before becoming a judge in California. In 1968, President Lyndon B. Johnson appointed her a federal appeals judge for the Ninth Circuit. Many thought she would become the first female Supreme Court judge if a slot had opened up. Instead, years later, President Carter asked Hufstedler to give up her lifetime appointment in the courts to take on the new role as secretary of education.

The department was not a popular one and was even considered, by some at the time, to be unconstitutional. Hufstedler focused on building the department and cementing relationships with the states as well as creating equality in education. She did both so well that the DOE is still in existence today. At the end of her term, in an open letter to her successor, she wrote that lots of people will debate education, but not many are willing to take a stand for kids. The job of the DOE Secretary is to "fight forcefully and joyfully" for kids.

Robert Slavin *and* Cooperative Learning

Dr. Robert Slavin's research showed that when high-performing students were teamed up with lower-performing students in small groups, everyone succeeded. Rather than divide kids into tracks based on grade level and learning abilities, where lower-performing kids tend to have fewer academic expectations, Slavin suggested putting learning groups together, rewarding the whole group when they do well, and then grading everyone individually. The result was that the high-performing students continued to make good grades and the students who struggled did better and understood the material quicker.

With his wife, Slavin created Success for All, an initiative originally rolled out in Baltimore, but that was then shared nationwide. It involved cooperative learning, tutoring, and parental and family assistance with health and nutrition. Slavin believed that evidence could back reform in education to create transformative change.

I Look Them in the Eye

Ms. Jessica Hawk

NEW JERSEY
HIGH SCHOOL AP ENGLISH, FILM STUDIES

They have burdens that I cannot see, and I want to be cognizant of that at all times.

There's a certain confidence that comes from being a "veteran" teacher—being past year five, or even year ten. In the beginning, because I was so desperate to prove myself and prove that I was a teacher, I wasn't as open to criticism, whether helpful or not. I wasn't as open to admitting mistakes because I did not want to look like a novice or be vulnerable. But then there comes a certain point when you say, "Okay, I'm established, and it is more than okay if I don't know something, if I need to work through something, if a lesson bombs, if somebody noticed something and needed to give me a gentle correction." That realization really made my teaching flourish. That's when I wasn't trying to play teacher anymore; I *was* a teacher.

Humor helps me motivate the kids. I come from a very funny family—we're always trying to out-yuck each other—so I come by it naturally. And when I'm in front of people, at this point in my life, I'm very confident. I'm self-assured and I love to joke, and I love to make people laugh. That's from the little-girl me who was insecure, who thought that if people were laughing with me, they weren't laughing at me. So, I developed a strong sense of humor.

I remember my teachers who were funny more than I remember any other teacher. I'm so lucky that we have a lot of hilarious teachers at my school. We motivate each other. I don't want to be the one class where the kids come in and go, "That was so boring."

I am so grateful that at the age of fifty-five these kids still want to engage with me. I don't take that for granted. I do believe it is based on the way that I treat them and the fact that I do want to listen to them. I can still remember what it was like to be them. I remember very clearly what it was like to have teen angst and anxiety. I didn't have a lot of self-confidence when I was younger. I had a wonderful teacher my junior year of high school named Mrs. Lane, and I would get to school early to talk to her (and now I realize, bother her, because she was probably there trying to get work done). She never made me feel as if I was imposing. So now if a kid comes to me, and I have so much to grade or so much to do, I just stop and tell myself, *This student is seeking your advice or your attention. Put your pen down.* And I look them in the eye.

A lot of connection moments like this came from the fact that I founded the Gay Straight Alliance at the school where I teach. In 1996, I had a really quiet student who sat in my class every day. He would nod and do his thing and never really said anything to me. Then one day, as he was leaving, he gave me a little, intricately folded note, and said, "Read this later." I immediately had to teach another class. So I had this note on my desk, and I was just dying to read it. When I finally got to my lunch, I opened it. He'd written, "I appreciate your class and what you're doing, and you're funny . . . I'm so happy to be in your class. Love, [his name]." And then he put, "PS: I'm gay." My heart stopped.

The next morning, I went to his homeroom and called him out. I said, "Can I see him in the hallway, please?" He came out the door panicking. I just said, "Congratulations!" and I hugged him. "That is not a postscript," I told him. "That's a script, and when you're ready, please make that script as loud as everything else. I don't know when you're going to be ready, but I am here."

In 2004–2005, when another one of my students came up to me and said, "I just went to a conference, and I want to start a Gay Straight Alliance and you're going to help me," I said yes. We have our twentieth anniversary this year.

I teach AP senior lit. One of the novels that I teach is called *The Things They Carried*. When I tell the kids it's a Vietnam War–era novel, they go, "Ehhhh . . ." I ask them, "Have you trusted me? Have I made good decisions for you so far? Will you trust me with this one?" One of the reasons I really love this book is because we're so far removed from that era at this point in time, and I think it's important for kids to understand the toll that war and conflict take on people for decades and generations. It's also important for my students to realize that everybody's carrying around intangible weight.

I take that philosophy when kids walk into my room. They have burdens that I cannot see, and I want to be cognizant of that at all times. I have some kids I say hello to every day at the door and they don't say hello back. I can't get my shorts in a twist about that and say, "Oh, that is about me." Not everything's about me. As they walk in, I think about them all wearing wet wool coats. They're cranky, the coat is itchy; it's uncomfortable. My goal throughout their time in my classroom is to get them to peel off the wet wool coat.

More Than a Teacher

Mr. Diego Napoles

CALIFORNIA
FOURTH GRADE GENERAL EDUCATION

A key phrase to tell kids is, "I've got time."

I wanted to be a musician when I was twenty-one. I wanted to be a producer; that's what my vision was for my life. I started teaching guitar to kids because I just needed a job, but then I found I really liked working with kids who were ten or eleven years old. There was one kid in particular who just felt so natural to work with. Even though we only met for twenty minutes a day after school to practice guitar, we talked about things outside of music—his other interests and his life. He would say things like, "My teachers don't believe in me." But then one day, he said to me, "Mr. Diego, I wish you were my dad." That was a crazy moment for me as a twenty-one-year-old. It felt so monumental, to see the impact that I could have on a kid's life, to be a positive male role model. That's what sparked it, my realization that I wanted to become a teacher.

It's sad because that kid reached out to me on social media years later when he was fourteen or fifteen, and he wasn't doing too well. I wrote back, saying, "Come visit me. I'm at the school down the street," but he never came. There are those moments where you wonder, *What more could I have done to help these students?* I think about that often.

I work in a low socioeconomic area, and in my nine years of teaching I've seen so many things, a lot of them deeply troubling. I've done my best to not become numb to it. Even if it's my ninetieth time hearing a similar

93

story, it's that kid's life and their foundation and their trauma they're going through currently. At the same time, when I go home and talk to my wife at night, it's hard not to feel like I can never do enough, like there aren't enough hours in the day. As a teacher, there's so much pressure about the academic aspects, which *are* essential. But at the same time, a kid who can read at grade level but doesn't have the social awareness to deal with their emotions is going to have a harder time than a kid who can't read but can cope with their anger, frustration, and depression. Those coping skills aren't apart of the standard yet, but they should be.

I tell myself I just have to do the best I can with what I have. The kid I taught guitar to? I know that at the time I tried my best and did what I could, and there's peace in that. Being grounded and aware is important for me. I feel I sleep better at night when I know I did everything I could.

Over a decade in the classroom, it's gotten easier for me to connect with kids. After time, you have practice, and you know what to look for and what to say in certain situations. There are so many little nuances, but here's the CliffsNotes version. A key phrase to tell kids is, "I've got time." They're so used to hearing that adults, especially the males in their lives, don't have time for them. So being very direct and letting them know that you do have time for them could be very important.

I also try to never say, "It's going to get better"—because I don't know if it's going to get better. What if I said that and then the kid had something even more traumatic happen?

The third part is empathy—letting them know that while you may not understand exactly what they're going through, you understand their emotions and their emotions are valid. For example: "It's okay to cry; I know you miss your dad." Boys especially need to know that they don't need to tough it out. I want to be a male role model in their lives saying it's okay to feel sadness and anger.

The last piece is saying, "Hey, I'm gonna go play football. You want to come and join?" Interaction outside of the classroom helps so much. Sometimes, a very deep part of the kid's connection to an adult—especially, for example, the connection between a boy and a dad—is just catching a baseball.

One of the treasures I keep on my desk is a note one of my students wrote. The kids were making valentines. I showed them pictures and told them stories about my daughter, so some of the kids were making her valentines too. That night, when my wife was reading them to our daughter, she found one that said, "You have the coolest dad. I wish your dad was my dad." I have that note on my desk. It's a kind of memento for those days when I'm feeling really stressed. When I'm at my desk, I can look over and see photos of my wife and my daughter, and then that note. It's a reminder that I can be someone who makes school a better place, a place they want to come to. It's a reminder that for these kids I have to be more than a teacher.

Finding the Right Combination

Mr. Sean Connolly

PENNSYLVANIA

ELEMENTARY SCHOOL
LEARNING SUPPORT AND GIFTED

I will definitely cry on some of my kids' last day of school because I just know them so well.

I don't know why, but at a certain point, I decided to go into teaching. One teacher suggested I get dual certified for special education because it would make me more marketable. Today, I've never had any other job but special ed. It wasn't really my goal at first, but it worked out.

For some reason everyone thinks it's so cool to come to my room. Some kids even ask me, "Mr. Connolly, can you take me too?" I'm the only learning support teacher in my school, and I teach gifted too. I have kids who are really struggling to read in fourth grade. I have a girl in third grade who's on a high school math level—she's smarter than me. Then I have other kids who are just so brilliant in other ways. Certain kids seem smart but maybe not gifted—then you give them different puzzles and they figure them out in seconds. It's a range, and it's fun.

Since I'm the only learning support teacher, I've had some of my students since kindergarten. I know their parents so well, and sometimes I know their grandparents. I work with them in such a different capacity than the classroom teachers do. I will definitely cry on some of my kids' last day of school because I just know them so well.

There's a reason they come to you—because they've been identified to have ADHD, autism, or a specific learning disability in math or writing or reading, for example. Your mindset changes so much; you realize that while students can be really behind, they can still do a lot of things; you just have to find the right combination to help them. It puts things in perspective. Sometimes kids are really struggling, and you feel like you've done the same thing hundreds of times. But sometimes it takes hundreds of reps for them to get it. It will click; it just takes a while. That's why I like working with kids when they're younger. You get to see their progress over time.

I have one fifth grader who met his learning goals. Now he says, "You don't ever take me anymore." And I'm like, "Yeah, that's good." It's a sad thing, because they're not coming to you anymore—but that's the goal, right?

Teaching is my passion—finding different things that work with kids. I used to write songs with my gifted kids; we'd rework the lyrics of pop songs to incorporate in lessons. It became this huge positive thing, and then everyone would work together to create songs. I had all these kids coming to me saying they wrote a song about math or another subject. We meet once or twice a week at a community center to sing them. The parents were obsessed with it. The kids were obsessed with it. Everyone had fun, and some of the kids were really talented singers. It's all about finding ways that kids can connect with the content.

When I started my first elementary job, my principal observed me in class. She said, "I love the way you just go in, and you don't care what you had planned or what you were going to do. You have no ego. You'll just change up everything to help the kids understand." And it's true: I have no interest in teaching kids things that they can't follow. I'll adapt for them; we'll go backwards if we need to.

It will click; it just takes a while.

A Safe Environment

Ms. Meghan Matulewicz

VIRGINIA

HIGH SCHOOL
PE AND HEALTH

I'm your teacher, and then I'm your coach and your mentor.

My first few months of teaching were really hard because I tried to go by the book. The other teachers didn't interact with the students. I was twenty-one and a brand-new teacher. I figured I would play it safe and follow the other teachers' lead. After about six months of trying that, I decided I was going to do what felt natural for me. I'm going to play with the kids and I'm going to ask them questions about things outside of school. A simple question like, "What did you have for dinner last night?" tells me so much because that can go into, "Well, my mom works late so I cooked for my siblings." That's when I fell in love with teaching—when I decided to do what other teachers didn't do.

A teacher I follow on social media has this motto of "to be cringe is to be free." I've developed that mindset. I'm your teacher; I'm not trying to impress you. You need to have confidence, and I just own it with them, and they still humble me all the time. But I think it makes that relationship so much stronger. It's okay that your teachers are going to mess up; we're going to make mistakes.

The most interesting part of health class is when we get into what's called family life; it used to be sex education. I only taught the female students as a female teacher, and I had a great rapport with them; they were comfortable with me, and they felt safe. I made it fun. I dyed water red to show them how tampons worked. I got granny panties from Walmart and put them on over my pants to show them how to put a pad on. They'd laugh, but I knew half of them were going to benefit from it. So many students who weren't mine came up to me to say they didn't get to do that in their class. They'd say, "They just showed us a picture." I want to be a hands-on person. That's just the type of teacher I am.

When we talk about STDs and birth control, I could look at my students and know who was sexually active and who had no idea what anything was. And then you have another student who still believes in Santa. And they're in the same class sitting at the same table. That's where I need to adapt and adjust, to realize that some students are hearing this for the very first time from me and not their parents. It can be emotional for people. I want to be the person who the students want to ask questions in a class discussion like that. The girls freely raise their hands, but I always hand out little pieces of paper if they want to write their questions down. Then they put them in a bucket to keep it anonymous. I would have maybe two people write stuff down. That's a win for me right there—that they're comfortable not only with me, but the students have felt that it's a safe environment for themselves and their classmates to ask those questions so openly.

Being a younger teacher has been a huge benefit for me. It was also a concern: Will they respect me still if I play around with them a little bit? I think I've done a good job with saying, first and foremost, "I'm your teacher, and then I'm your coach and your mentor." I never want it to be like we're friends because that's not it. I make that very clear.

Getting the Ship Together

Ms. Laura Pitts

GEORGIA

ELEMENTARY SCHOOL
KINDERGARTEN/ESOL

★ Being a teacher means putting the students first.

When I am one hundred years old, on my deathbed, and someone asks me, "What was it like being a teacher?" I will think about the year that one of my students, Miles, was killed very suddenly in a crash early in the school year. It was the most transformative touchpoint year of my life—not just my life as a teacher, but my life as a person—the way that losing a student affected me and affected the rest of the class.

I credit a lot of how I responded, especially in those early moments, to my parents and the kind of people that they are and the kind of person they taught me to be. When my friend and one of Miles's neighbors called to tell me about the crash, I didn't have to stop to think. I ran up to the hospital to see what was going on. I felt like my mom, sitting in that ER waiting room, passing out little clementines to the other kids who were there for their sick sibling or cousin. That's just what you do. Helping Miles's family in the hospital that night, that's just what you do.

When Miles died, we were all in mourning and shock. I felt like the captain of a ship that went so tragically off course. The kids were traumatized. The parents of the kids were traumatized. I became so close to the parents in that class because I knew they were depending on me and our class paraprofessional, Ms. Rachael, to keep some semblance of normality, comfort, and safety for their kids, and to also get them ready for first grade. Ms. Rachael kept Miles as a part of our classroom community by laminating his picture and giving one to all of the students. I ran into one of those students this fall and she said she still has that picture in her room.

When I think about that year, I'll never forget the very last day of school that May. I live really close to school, and as I drove up the hill, I just started bawling. I had done what I could do for those children who were so lost in mourning, and I had strived to support all the families. That day, it was a feeling of relief—not a good feeling of relief, but a realization that somehow, I made it through this year of keeping our little ship together. The parents gave me a little heart-shaped stepping stone that I put on my front porch. It has all of the kids' names on it. Every day when I come into my house, I see their names and Miles's name, and I think about them.

Miles was killed the week before we were set to have our first parent-teacher conferences. A few weeks after he died, I scheduled one with Miles's parents and went to their house to have it. From years of conferencing with kindergarten parents, I know that to get insight into who they are in a school community is everything. I've found that the overwhelming majority of parents just want to know if their child was kind. How did they treat their teachers and their classmates? That's part of the magic of kindergarten. For parents, it's often their first experience getting feedback on who their child is in a classroom community. I knew that for Miles's parents to hear insight that he was a great friend and people loved sitting next to him, that he was funny, would be so special.

I'm no longer a classroom teacher. Now, I'm on a team working with English language learners. It has been really invigorating for my career to be able to do a different kind of work this year. But it also makes me realize that being a classroom teacher is the hardest job in the world. Being a teacher means putting the students first, even in life and death situations, and knowing it's your job to keep them calm because it can impact their lives forever.

They were depending on me and Ms. Rachael to keep some semblance of normality, comfort, and safety for their kids.

Everything brings a sparkle to their eyes. They help me keep the sparkle for my own life.

— JUAN GONZALEZ

YOU always remember the teachers who inspired you. Those teachers found a way to connect you with the subject matter that no one had been able to before. Maybe they sparked your love of reading with the right book at the right time, or ignited your creativity with a challenging project they trusted you could do. Maybe they found just the right way to explain chemistry to make you realize you were actually, surprisingly (to you), interested in the subject.

Teachers who are passionate about what they teach naturally inspire. Their love of the subject matter is infectious, and their excitement to share it turns kids into partners of learning. That inspiration is a two-way street, by the way. Inspired kids inspire teachers too—to create, to keep exploring, to show up again and again.

They Inspire

Changing the Game: Sparking Inspiration

Georgette Yakman *and* STEAM

Working as a middle school and high school technology teacher, Georgette Yakman covered STEM—science, technology, engineering, and mathematics—topics with her students daily in the classroom. But in 2006, she tried something different. She added an A: the arts. Yakman felt that weaving the humanities into STEM education fit better with how people learned, giving them a human connection to the subject matter. As Yakman puts it, the A isn't adding another subject to tackle; it's a way to knit all the subjects together. She considers the humanities to be the context for the logical reasoning presented by the STEM disciplines.

Once Yakman put STEAM—sometimes written as STΣ@M—into practice in 2007, interest in the framework increased. By 2011, South Korea had adopted the STEAM framework nationwide, and Yakman's work had been recognized with several awards.

Jane Elliott *and the* "Blue Eyes/Brown Eyes" Experiment

On April 5, 1968, Jane Elliott split her third grade classroom into two groups. The blue-eyed kids would move to one side of the room, and the nonblue-eyed kids would go to the other. It was the day after Martin Luther King Jr. had been shot in Memphis, Tennessee, and Elliott, teaching in Riceville, Iowa, wanted her kids to understand what racism and prejudice felt like.

Segregated by a random trait they had no control over, the blue-eyed kids were told they were inferior to the other kids, and their classroom rights were curtailed. The next day, the roles were reversed. The blue-eyed kids were now superior to their peers, with the dark-eyed children now relegated to second-class status.

Known as the "Blue Eyes/Brown Eyes" experiment, Elliott's two-day lesson helped kids understand racism on a visceral level and inspired many others to bring that experiential learning into the classroom.

Anne Carroll Moore *and* Children's Libraries

Believe it or not, kids under the age of fourteen often weren't allowed in libraries in the late 1800s. All that changed thanks to Anne Carroll Moore's advocacy. She wrote a proposal outlining what children's libraries could look like—spaces filled with kids' books and helmed by librarians well-versed in children's literature. In 1906, she became the head of the children's library at the New York Public Library (NYPL). In that role, she mentored other librarians in children's services and created many popular programs. By 1913, kids' books accounted for one third of all books borrowed from the NYPL.

Aha Moments

Mr. Juan Edgar Gonzalez Jr.

TEXAS

THIRD GRADE
ENGLISH AND SOCIAL STUDIES

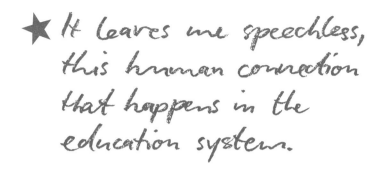

It leaves me speechless, this human connection that happens in the education system.

When I started college, my first semester, I got really sick. I had non-Hodgkins lymphoma cancer, and it was at stage four when they found it. I went through chemotherapy; I went through radiation. I was super young, going through this deadly experience. When I came back from it, I started to rethink life—*What is it that I want to do?*—and teaching was at the top.

At the elementary level, it's so pure at this age. Everything is amazing. Everything brings a sparkle to their eyes. They help me keep the sparkle for my own life. It's the human aspect of it that I think makes teaching so exciting. And then the academic side of it—really getting to see what the brain can do. Third grade is the sweet spot for me. They're still young and everything I say wows them, but they can handle things and can have conversations and ask questions.

I always give them the why. If I'm talking about how I'm doing classroom management or how I expect them to walk in the hallway, it's never just that, "I'm your teacher and this is what I want from you." Giving them the why allows them to understand, "Oh, so that's why we have to be quiet in the hallway, because it's a safety concern. You're not just trying to control me." I look to give them the why when it comes to academics too. I really give them the opportunity to understand how genres work— why this is fiction, why this is nonfiction, and how our brain reads these things differently. The why is rarely built into our curriculum. Rather than just giving them the standard and trying to see if they can summarize this piece of text, I want to build a foundation. For me, giving students the why always brings the aha moment.

I love picture books. I love sharing. I love that they're a short journey. I love reading aloud. I'm working with so many different students—students who are innate readers, who are dyslexic, who are still reading below grade level—but when I read to them, all that evens out, whether we're reading a chapter book or a picture book.

The books I share with my students cover a broad range. I want students to be able to know there are so many different types of stories that exist. I have this rule that I'm not going to be the teacher who just reads *Charlotte's Web* because it's a third grade novel. I'm going to find new novels. *The Wild Robot* series by Peter Brown is such a phenomenal series. It captures what I love most about literacy—really great characters, amazing life lessons, and it makes me think about my life. The conversations with my students are deep—they get it, and they fall in love with the characters the same way that I have. When I can hit a home run with a book like that—where I know it's going to touch many lives and it's not just reflective of one person's life—those are my favorites to share. It allows me to show them the world where they can see themselves but also learn something.

My ultimate goal, more than standards, more than anything else, is, "How do I get you on the path to being a reader?" Nothing makes me happier than when parents tell me their kids are asking to go to the library or to buy a book when they've never done that before. It's human nature to want stories. You just need that home run book, the one that's gonna strike that match and make them think, "What have I been missing out on? I need to keep reading."

I showcase my reading to my students. I show them, "Look what I checked out at the library," "Look what book I just purchased," or, "Look what books someone gave to me." I'm showcasing my reading and writing life so that they see it can exist outside of this academic work that we do. That way, they can start to find little nooks and crannies in their own life and start self-identifying as a writer or reader. So when they do leave me and I'm no longer with them, at least I've started building those foundations.

I've done this long enough that high schoolers are coming back and what they are most likely to say when they come to me is: "I remember when you read this book and now, I'm reading this book." When I really think about it, it reaffirms this idea of, *Wow, you really are part of someone's life*. You're not just this little thing that happens for a year and then they move on. They hold on to these memories. Still, after so many years, it leaves me speechless, this human connection that happens in the education system.

I don't ever want to talk so optimistically about teaching and make it feel like I'm not aware of the struggles that teachers are going through because I see them and go through them too. When the time is right, it's important to tell those stories. But let's not forget the good stories too because that's what's keeping us here, and that's what brought us here.

A Special Form of Education

Ms. Jere Chang

ATLANTA

ELEMENTARY SCHOOL
GIFTED

You're gonna need a little support, and that's okay.

I will tell you this; if you're bored and you start teaching kindergarten, it will cure your boredom, hands down. I fell in love with their enthusiasm for learning.

What I wasn't prepared for was the micromanagement. I think part of it was the cultural-shock shift for me, but I was miserable. So I became intentional. I got a third master's degree, and I intentionally sought out a school that I felt would be a good fit for me.

Gifted education is on the chopping block in some states. Are there issues in gifted education with identifying giftedness? Absolutely. There are cultural biases and definitely issues with identifying Black and brown kids. There are ongoing conversations that we need to continue to have to be equal. Even the word *gifted* is problematic. It triggers a lot of people, but I think it's misunderstood. I define *gifted* as the students who are accelerated in one or more academic areas. Even teachers misunderstand it. They'll say, "Why are they gifted? They don't do anything in my class." But not all gifted kids are highly motivated. As a matter of fact, many of them are not motivated at all. There's this stereotype among a lot of people that all gifted kids are high achieving and highly motivated, but that cannot be farther from the truth. The pressures that parents/teachers place on this label "gifted" are problematic.

In Georgia, gifted education is under the umbrella of special education, as it should be. It is a special form of education. My kids are gifted in a lot of different areas. I do creativity activities and then logical awareness, divergent thinking, and more throughout the day. We'll do a creative activity and a third of my kids will say it's their favorite. Then we'll do something more mathematically minded, where there's a right and wrong answer, and another third will prefer that. And we talk about how, throughout the school day, there are going to be things that you have to do that you just don't like. I tell them it's the same with me: There are parts of my job I don't like. But I love creating and being creative.

I have a kid who's a creative thinker and hates math. When we do the creative activity, I tell him, "Hey, this is your time to shine. Go for it—show off a little bit," and then I will celebrate that kid. When we get to more of the logical thinking, I tell him, "You're gonna need a little support, and that's okay. Let's find that support because you've got to get through those things that you don't like in school. It's just a part of the process."

I definitely have more freedom than some of the general education teachers. My standards are creativity, divergent thinking, research skills, and collaboration, and they're very loosely written as opposed to a fourth grade teacher's standards. It's just more black and white, and my standards are quite gray.

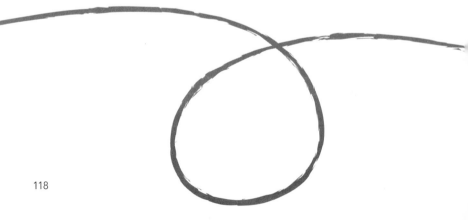

My favorite unit that I totally wrote by myself and did all the research for—I think it's fire, or whatever young people say—is how to increase awareness of diversity in the race to space. We spend the entire first semester learning about celestial bodies, planets, Pluto not being a planet, and all that. We become experts in space, if you will. Then for the second semester, all we do is learn about people who have helped us explore space. And the one thing that these people have in common is that they're all Black people. Most folks have never heard of them, aside from the ones in *Hidden Figures*—Dorothy Vaughan, Mary Jackson, and Katherine Johnson. There's Mae Jemison, the first Black astronaut woman in space. Ron McNair, an astronaut and physicist. Leland Melvin— he played professional football for the Detroit Lions, and then became an astronaut. Victor Glover, who's getting ready to orbit the moon. He'll be the first Black person to orbit, and these kids have never heard of him.

To have that support from my school and community to be so intentional about Black education and representation makes me feel very fortunate. To be able to deviate from some of the standards of who the state deems as important that the kids learn about—it's going to be John Glenn, Buzz Aldrin, and yes, those folks deserve their props—but to go beyond that and offer kids that representation? It's one of my favorite projects.

Helping Kids Fall in Love with Learning

Ms. Vesa Ahiyya

OREGON

KINDERGARTEN
GENERAL EDUCATION

I come from a whole line of educators. My great-grandfather was the principal, teacher, bus driver, probably janitor too, at a school in Mesquite, Texas. He was an educator during segregation, from 1940 up till the 1970s. The oldest of his nine children was my grandfather. He went on to join the army, but when he retired, he started teaching. He was married to my grandmother, who taught first grade for years. And my mother started teaching when she was about eighteen (she graduated college really early) and married my father, who was also in the military, then retired and became a teacher. My aunt is a teacher . . . Everyone's a teacher. Education has always been a part of my life, which is why when I went to college, I absolutely wanted *nothing* to do with it. I went to college as premed, with plans to be a brain surgeon or work in pediatrics. Then I failed my first biology course. When I called my mom, she said to me, "I know you don't want to. But what if you tried an education class?"

I took my first education course, and the professor was incredible. At 8 a.m., she was bubbly, ready to go, and so passionate about education. I thought, *If anything, I just want to be like that—excited about what I'm doing.* I got my start in a little red school as one of two kindergarten teachers and I loved it. I loved being with kids that young, and I loved helping kids fall in love with learning.

★ Stories help kids see themselves and their peers, and to celebrate each other's differences.

Kindergarten is definitely challenging, but I think it's the most magic you'll see in 180 days. What's exciting is that you get to give these kids their first experiences; you're giving them their launching pad. So even with its challenges, it's magical. As a kindergarten teacher, you get to say, "Let's make school a safe place for you. Let's make sure you understand." You get kids from all over and you build this community with them. You put all your hopes and wishes and dreams into them, and then you shove them off to first grade and hope that first grade teacher sees their curiosity and loves the silly, goofy stuff they say as much as you do.

I really do believe that learning should be fun. I don't necessarily believe that our education system right now is a lot of fun. But I do believe that learning—the process of getting and retaining information—should be fun. When I moved from Austin to Boston, I lost a little bit of the fun. I lost a bit of myself in that transition. The school in Boston was a space where I was told, "We don't really do that here. That is not how we do things." So I started wearing a tutu. It was my subtle, nice way of saying, "I'm gonna do me. I'm gonna close my door, and I'm gonna do what I know is best for kids." Which is to always keep the idea of the individual while working in a community. In other words, saying, "Who you are is respected and cared for and loved in this space. We're gonna learn our ABCs and have important conversations around a myriad of topics, but this will always be a space where your self is always valued." The tutu is a representation of that.

I love reading, but when I became a teacher, I had a very pitiful library, so I had to build. My school was a dual language school and we really had to think about getting texts in other languages. I had about seven or eight different languages in the classroom, and I wanted some books that were either in the languages of the kids at the very least, or that represented their culture and experiences. I had Russian, Castilian, German, and Japanese, but I did not have a library that was going to make a kid see themselves in a story. Which is especially important in kindergarten—you want them to fall in love with stories and not just *Good Night Moon*. I needed books that would motivate them to continue that search for stories and that love of reading.

That's when I really started zooming in and focusing on the lack of stories. It was a time when society was realizing most of the characters in kids' books were either animals or white. That's where my passion started. When I became an author, I really wanted a kid to be able to say, "Oh, yeah, that's kind of like me," and not me as the writer but as the people in the story. The characters in my stories might show nontypical behavior or learn differently.

I was really excited about a kid sitting in our library with a book in their lap and being able to say, "We do this at my home too." I vividly remember two kids who were both Jewish, sitting down with a book and saying, "This is how we do Hanukkah. This looks like our dreidel." Having that conversation should be an opportunity for every kid.

Kindergarten has this range where some kids, by the end of their time, are reading chapter books, and some kids are just finally able to write their name. Both of those journeys are important and matter. We always hear about the kids who learn to read. We also need to celebrate the kids who learn how to tie their shoelaces. That's growth too, and that matters too. It just looks different. Stories help kids see themselves and their peers, and to celebrate each other's differences—that learning to read is amazing, and that sometimes just learning to tie their shoes is amazing too.

Hope for the Future

Mr. Zachary
Lombardi

NEW YORK

ELEMENTARY SCHOOL
VISUAL ARTS

Maybe they'll mess up twenty times, but they know they can do it, because they're done it before.

I wanted to be an artist, a sculptor—that was my main thing in high school and beforehand. But what does the path of being an artist look like? Through art school, it started to seem a little selfish of me to say, "Oh, I'm just going to make art for myself all the time." It seemed kind of nice to pass the skill around a little bit. Teaching seemed like a good job—a good, safe bet. And then when I started, I just fell in love with it.

When I took the job at this school in Staten Island, they hadn't had an art teacher for twenty years. It was my chance to start the art program from scratch. I'm also a sustainability coordinator for my school—I'm trying to make the art program fund itself by using garbage as art supplies. We go to reuse centers and pick stuff out of the trash. Everything's recycled. For our art show, everything was made out of old newspaper and cardboard. The core value of the art program is a collaborative problem-solving design process, and I can teach that using anything really.

I teach pre-K through fifth grade. The level of progression you get to see is just insane. In pre-K, they can't write the alphabet. Then, before you know it, they're writing a novel for the Ezra Jack Keats Bookmaking Project and their book is being displayed in Manhattan. The amount of change a kid goes through, from someone who comes in in September and cries every day and is scared to leave home to this independent being in fifth grade is amazing—and as a teacher, you see the whole thing.

It's very nice to teach every day. It's not easy—and crazy things happen—but it's mostly pretty happy. Kids are a lot easier than adults. They're happy to be there. Even when we have one day left of school before summer break, they're still coming in. They're ready to make art. They build you up.

The teaching profession is intrinsically optimistic. To do this job, a career and life's work, there has to be, in the back of your head, hope for the future. Otherwise, you really shouldn't be doing it if you don't think that those kids are going to be a better version of you. If you don't think they can be the next leaders of the country, then why go into teaching? Everyone says, "Oh, this generation. There's too much technology. We're doomed." I disagree. These kids can do so much more than I could at their age, and it's great.

The studio space is important to me. You have conversations with each other. Being around the work of other people can shift the work you're doing, change your opinion of things, or just get you interested and excited about something you maybe wouldn't have found without them. That's what I like to have in my classroom. Seeing all these kids making art in my classroom, building things together, and working collaboratively . . . being in that setting just gets me so jazzed to make sculpture. One group of friends made a dragon out of garbage that's seven feet long. Nothing makes me feel like I did my job more than seeing four boys team up and do that all by themselves.

Kids are excited about things in a different way than a lot of adults are. It's not that adults aren't curious, but they're not curious the way kids are. The kids bring you back every day. They get you out of zombie-mode and ready to go back home, go into your own studio, and make stuff.

The problem-solving kids get to experience in the visual arts is one of the greatest skills you can give them in life. There's not a cut-and-dry answer to a lot of what you're doing. When the kids are building large sculptures and creating crazy prints, there are techniques that they're learning like any other subject. But to create, you have to constantly tackle problems and fail, and then try again. And they're doing that every time they come into the art room.

It doesn't matter if you're going to be in the art or design world. What you learn in the art room translates into any career you're going to choose. In art class, kids learn how to be a flexible person who knows that they can tackle something and figure it out. Maybe they'll mess up twenty times, but they know they can do it, because they've done it before, and they've seen that they can make something if they just keep at it. That's what the visual arts really gives to the kids.

The amount of change a kid goes through . . . as a teacher, you see the whole thing.

The Energy of Teaching

Ms. Lindsay Nichols

MAINE
HIGH SCHOOL
BIOLOGY AND ANATOMY/PHYSIOLOGY

If you're passionate about what you do, you're always thinking about it.

I want students to walk in my door and say, "Thank god, it's biology!" I start every class blasting music, everyone from Taylor Swift to the Rolling Stones, and a lot of times, kids will come in dancing. We're going to have fun and we're going to learn and it's going to be explorative, not stagnant.

I've been teaching for twenty years, and when I first started it was about the content—I had to make sure students knew the content. Now I look at teaching very differently. I want to build personalities and inspire people through the content.

For me, I look at teaching as an entertainer through the lens of biology. Think about when you go to a concert or a play: If it's not good, you want to leave. When I think about framing a lecture, I think about how I can make it a moment of experience. When you think about a memory you had as a kid, there was something that happened that branded that experience and helped it stay with you. How do I do that for the concept of homeostasis? How do I do that for the concept of protein synthesis?

I try to work with vivid imagery for the big-ticket items I want them to learn. To brand a concept like homeostasis—which is kind of like a figure-eight showing how we regulate our body temperature, our blood sugar—I'll show them a picture of elephant ears. They'll think, "How do elephant ears relate to this?" But then, at any point later in the school year, I can say, "Elephant ears," and they'll say, "Oh, homeostasis." For the lesson about invasive species, an important concept in ecology, I start by playing AC/DC's "Thunderstruck" with a video of a crab running on a treadmill. That crab happens to be the very invasive green crab off the coast of Maine. It's entertainment, and a lot of times, they don't even know that they're learning. But it takes a lot of preparation to do it that way.

If you're passionate about what you do, you're always thinking about it. How can I make this better? How can I make that bigger for them, so it seems more meaningful? It's just constant reflection. When you walk out of the classroom, you don't stop thinking about what you teach, who you're impacting, who's sitting in front of you. Standing up in front of teenagers is not easy. You've got a lot of personalities. Some of them are completely disengaged and want nothing to do with you. How do you bring them all in? I'll wake up in the middle of the night thinking, *How do I get this kid engaged in some way?*

One of the most important things is to become part of a student's life, to find something that drives them, and to make sure that they think *you think* it's important. What are they passionate about? It could be one tiny thing—say they love horses. You just ask them about it and their faces get brighter. They feel like they matter, and they do. That's what I want students to understand when they walk in my classroom: that they matter. I care about you. I want you to learn and love biology. But I want you to feel like you're cared for in this classroom. I think students will work for you if they feel that they're cared for. That's the energy of teaching. They don't want to be there in the beginning, so how can you get 95 percent of them to love being in your classroom by the end? You're not going to get everyone. I would be lying to you if I said I got every single student. But I'm okay with 95 percent.

The kids bring you back. The moments, the kids, the classes, the relationships you build, the collaboration that you see in every class . . . You look at where you started with a group of kids and the amount of energy it took to work through the year, and it's just an amazing product. The addictive piece about teaching is knowing that you've had that impact. You've taken a blank slate, and you've built this model of understanding. In my case, it's about biology, but it's more than just biology. It's life skills; it's building and maturing kids to be good people, to be part of their community, to inspire them so in the future they'll inspire and do good things for others.

It's your job to have a kid throw a chair at you, and then you've still got to love that kid and be there with them and teach them.

—JOSH MONROE

TEACHING isn't just about the lesson plan

or meeting standards. Kids don't walk in as blank slates ready to plug in and learn; they bring with them their feelings, experiences outside of school, and struggles. To be extraordinary teachers, educators must care about more than academics—they care for the whole child.

For many kids, their teachers are the first adults outside of their family to help them, cheer them on, see them for who they are, believe in who they will be, show up for them, and just plain love them. Teachers nurture their students' passions, encouraging them to explore topics and skills that make their eyes light up. They support their students through challenges, like struggling to read, and see them through big life changes, like a move or divorce. Sometimes, nurturing looks like letting an exhausted student nap at their desk or honoring their wish to be left alone with their feelings. Other times, nurturing is simply saying, "I love you."

They Nurture

Changing the Game: Caring for Kids

Vivian Gussin Paley *and* Encouraging Play

As a teacher in New Orleans in the 1950s, Vivian Gussin Paley started to wonder whether the emphasis on stringent rules and exacting lessons in early childhood education was the best way for her students to learn. In Great Neck, New York, and Chicago, Illinois, Paley noticed how the kindergartners engaged with each other and homed in on what she saw as two hugely important elements: play and the power of storytelling.

Paley began to harness her kindergartners' natural behaviors—playing, interacting, imagining, telling fantastic stories, and acting—as a way to help them learn and grow. She was known for saying, "You can't say you can't play." In the 1970s, Paley began to write about her observations in the classroom, eventually authoring more than a dozen books on early childhood development, including topics such as fairness, race, and social connection. Paley won several awards for her work, including a MacArthur Fellowship, and inspired educators through her work at the University of Chicago Laboratory.

Dr. James Comer *and the* Comer Model

The Comer Model, named after Dr. James Comer, is centered on the saying, "It takes a village to raise a child." Dr. Comer began to form the foundation of his model while doing an internship in his hometown in Indiana. He noticed that some of his friends had bad outcomes in life, despite having a similar academic background and sharing similar situations. He realized that it came down to different experiences at home.

In 1968, Dr. Comer was asked to lead a program through Yale University that focused on education creating better opportunities for Black kids. Working at two low-income schools in New Haven, Connecticut, Comer pulled together the efforts of the school staff, mental health staff, and parents into a cohesive and dynamic team all centered on the child's social and emotional needs. He also helped shift teachers' focus away from behaviors and onto the children. The results were amazing: The schools involved in the program eventually surpassed national performance standards.

Timothy Shriver and Dr. Roger P. Weissberg *and* Social-Emotional Learning

Working together with a team of teachers and researchers in the late 1980s, Timothy Shriver and Dr. Roger Weissberg built the framework for social-emotional learning. They were responding to New Haven superintendent John Dow Jr.'s aim for a focus on social development in all schools in the district.

Shriver, Weissberg, and their team created the New Haven Development Program, a curriculum for students in kindergarten through twelfth grade based on the idea that learning social and emotional skills would help reduce behavior issues in the classroom and better students' academic performance. Building on Dr. Comer's model, the study found that involving teachers, parents, mental health staff, other students, and community members helped students achieve the best outcomes.

Just Breathe

Ms. Erika Sandstrom

| MASSACHUSETTS |
| MIDDLE SCHOOL DIGITAL MEDIA |

They're excited to do it because they have the skills.

I've been teaching for thirty-three years. Yes, I still have yellow chalk underneath my fingernails.

For the past several years, I've been teaching something called Digital Media, which is a course that they let me create. I teach the kids about all the careers in animation, video production, music production, and so on. The green screen is a huge part of my class. Not because it's technology, but because of the social-emotional learning that naturally happens with it. In my class, the green screen is not about the kids taking the background out. You can do that many ways now. It's actually the experience it provides—of being on stage, being a director, being a set person, and being able to problem-solve together and work things out.

I do a lot of ridiculous things with them. First, we'll make videos that aren't really related to the curriculum, but that's how I teach them how to use these new tools. If I want them to learn how to do jump cuts, or how to use the green screen and all the animation you can do on it, we'll do a music video or something really silly. Then I'll say, "Now we're going to use this for a science project," and they're excited to do it because they have the skills. The healthiest thing kids and middle schoolers, and even adults, can do is play. Kids shouldn't be sitting in their seats. It's bad for their spines. We need to get them up and moving.

A powerful piece of who I am right now involves teaching mindfulness through creative media. I've been teaching yoga for over twenty years, and I've always been into mindfulness. I started a club called the Mindful Superhero Club, where I teach mindfulness to kids who come after school; we meditate, we do yoga, and then we make videos. One of them was about negative self-talk, how we put ourselves down. The kids wanted to put green capes on, and we used the capes as green screens and filled them with videos. In the final video, the Mindful Superheroes save the girl when she drops her books and starts calling herself an idiot. The kids came up with the catchphrase, "Put your brakes on that negative self-talk." We didn't show the video a ton because the kids didn't want to, but they told their friends about it. And then I heard kids in the hallway, who weren't in my class and who I don't even know, saying to each other, "Put your brakes on that negative self-talk over there."

Kids are sponges of energy. The world is chaotic right now, and our kids are just responding to the chaotic energy. We have wars going on; Jewish hate is back. I'm seeing fistfights in my school every day, which is something I've never seen before. With middle school, you know there's always something going on behind-the-scenes. Their behaviors aren't a personal attack. So when something happens, you have to think, *Oh, that poor babe. I'm going to send him love in his heart. Because right now something's going on with him. I don't know why he's walking on the tables and throwing cereal and shoving it up his nose. But I'm sure there's a reason.*

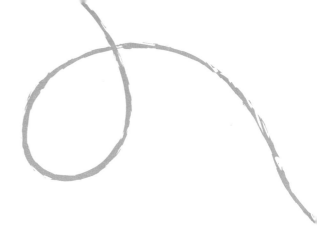

Also from yoga, breathing techniques got me through a lot of tough stuff in my life; once I saw how powerful it was, I dove into the science behind breathing. I use breathing bubbles a lot in my class. They're animations that expand and contract while you breathe along with them. One day I thought it would be cool if we could put something personal inside the breathing bubble, something that would bring you joy, like a picture of your cat. That is the one lesson plan that I get 100 percent participation in. I see the kids using their bubbles on their phones, and it's teaching them the power of breath.

I became a teacher for a negative reason that eventually turned into a positive. In high school, I had a creative writing teacher who almost failed me right before graduation. She kept comparing me to my older sister. She'd say, "You don't write like your sister. Do whatever you need to do to pass." It caused a lot of depression. Because of that, I decided I wanted to be a teacher because I didn't want any kid to ever experience what I experienced.

There's so much going on that affects them. That's why I teach them breathing. It is worth spending the time. I want to teach them video production, and we're also going to do something that's going to help them.

They're Becoming People

Ms. Julia Brown

I get to watch them grow up and see their interests change.

My mom was a middle school teacher. Being the child of an educator, life revolved around school and a lot of my life took place at school. I got my degree in early childhood education. Then I interned in kindergarten, but when they had a position open the next fall in kindergarten, I thought, *I don't know if I can do kindergarten all day.* So I decided to go to graduate school. The best advice I got was to do it in a different discipline in graduate school so I'd have some options. I always liked reading and going to the library at school, so I chose the path of a librarian.

Corduroy the teddy bear has become such a big part of our library. He is my child. I adopted him. One day toward the end of the year, I thought, *I don't know what to do with these kindergartners.* Then I walked in my office and there was a basket of stuffed animals, and Corduroy happened to be on top. So I grabbed him and told the kids, "Here's Corduroy. He's going to sit with whoever is doing a good job." It was a last-ditch effort, and they loved it. They worked so hard to have Corduroy sit at their table. At the end of the school year, they said, "What's Corduroy going to do? You can't just leave him here." So Corduroy came home with me and started his social media journey sharing all of the things he did that summer. We have Corduroy's birthday party. He gets Christmas presents from the kids. One little boy went to an Atlanta Braves game and bought Corduroy his own little baseball.

I see trends come and go. There have been years when we cannot keep *Diary of a Wimpy Kid* on the shelf, and now we have two full shelves of it. A lot of the little ones are interested in animals, but as they get older, boys often stick with nonfiction and girls like fiction/realistic fiction. However, they all cannot get enough scary stuff—everyone loves ghost stories. That shelf is always empty.

Interests change through the years. Boys will get to an age where they say to me, "Oh my gosh, you have car books and football books?" They start asking for books that connect to their life. When they get a little more confident, they want chapter books. Then there are some who I struggle to convince to check out a book. I love it when I finally find something they're interested in. "Do you like comic books?" "No." "Do you like animals?" "No." I keep going until they finally say, "Yeah . . . yeah!" This is why I do what I do.

When students are young, they're devastated if they can't check out a book one day. It's more challenging when they're older. To try to keep them engaged, I ask them for their input when I order books. I tell them, "I'm getting old. Who do y'all like? Who's famous now?" Sometimes I just put out chart paper and ask them to make me a list of things that they would read if I bought it.

I still believe with all of my heart that kids need to see themselves and their families in the stories they read. I remember, when I was a little girl, that Barbie was blonde, and most of the Disney princesses had blonde hair and blue eyes, except for Belle. I loved Belle because of her brown hair; she looked like me. Kids need to see characters who look like them. They need to see families that look like their families.

People don't really know how much goes into ordering books. We have standards and committees. Our orders have to be reviewed by a committee before we put them in, and then when the books come in, they physically have to be reviewed by a committee before we can put them into circulation. Many books at the high school level have been challenged in our district, and while I haven't had anything challenged, it does put me on edge. It feels like people are looking for you to do something wrong or trying to catch you with something they don't like. I haven't had to fight that fight, but it's one that I'm willing to fight for my students.

The beauty of being a special area teacher is that I have them year after year. We have four-year-olds all the way to ten-year-olds. I get to watch them grow up and see their interests change. I don't get to build the relationships as quickly or sometimes as deeply as their grade teachers. But I do like getting to see how they grow from tiny little kids. I see a lot of them mature from when they were such busy little preschoolers to . . . "Wow, they're becoming people."

Kids need to see themselves and their families in the stories they read.

A Culture of Introspection and Support

Mr. Jerome Hunter

Okay, there's a lot of stuff going on here, but it's also an opportunity.

I saw an opportunity in the town that I grew up in. There weren't a lot of male teachers, nor were there a lot of male teachers of color. And so, as I got older and went to college, I felt motivated to fill that void to the best of my ability and get into education. I also come from a blue-collar family where, typically, you work after high school; you don't necessarily go to college. I chose a different path to go to college and study and try to figure out what inspired me. What I learned was that human connection is really important.

Through my studies as an undergraduate, I was inspired by readings from Frederick Douglass, Malcolm X, Martin Luther King Jr., and some of the early activists around the importance of education. When I graduated, I was at a crossroads where I was deciding whether to go to law school or to get my master's in teaching. I saw the two professions as opportunities to make real inroads in changing the way we interact with one another in our society. I was reading Frederick Douglass, and there's a quote attributed to him, that, paraphrasing, says it's more impactful to mold the minds of the youth than it is to change the minds of older men. That was my indicator to hop into education and I haven't looked back.

I've come to realize that middle school is a time where the pilot lights are still on. As I gained experience and knowledge, I did some research and learned that middle school age, about ten-and-a-half to fourteen-and-a-half, is this time in our lives where there's significant physiological growth, neurological growth, and hormonal growth, and it's all crashing and converging. So we need to step back and look at it from an asset-based lens rather than a deficit-based lens—we need to say, "Okay, there's a lot of stuff going on here, but it's also an opportunity."

If we look at it from a gentle lens and take a gentler approach, we can help to support not only their academic growth, but also their holistic growth through those middle years and set them up for success in high school.

We make kids get in a row of seats. We say we're not going to have any outdoor time. We try to make everything very structured. But the natural response to that from any tweenager or teenager is pushback, and it creates this cycle of resistance. Instead, let's open up a little bit. Let's give them time to ask questions, explore, go outside a little bit, and normalize these developmental stages in their life. It allows them to take a beat, take a deep breath, relax their shoulders, and say, "Wait, this is normal, right?" For example, I've often told my students, "Know how sometimes it's hard for you to sit still?" And they say, "Yeah, what's that about?" Their bones are growing faster than their muscles and tendons. They don't need to feel as if this is a problem. It's just normal development.

Doing the same with emotions, specifically with boys, is helpful: "You might feel anxious, you might feel angry, you might feel sad, and all of those emotions are human and normal." If you can teach them to take a moment to try to recognize where they are in their brain, their response to that feeling could be different. It gives them a little bit of agency on how they approach the day. Obviously, it's easier said than done, but that's when naming it helps—and if you name it collectively and normalize it in an educational setting—it really creates a culture of introspection and collective support.

I have a specific focus on middle school boys because naming their emotions or naming what's going on with them is a way to socialize away from the attitude that they just have to suck it up, move on, and keep going. They hear that it's stupid for them to talk about their emotions, so they don't. But if a space is designated for this type of holistic learning, boys will participate. We see the challenges in our schools, in our society, with folks who identify as men and male, so what can we do to support them?

In middle school, the tenderness still exists. Middle school teachers still have a similar influence on their students as grade-school teachers do. There's still that nurturing element there. Middle school becomes the last stop.

Creating Community

Ms. Melody Munch

OKLAHOMA
SECOND GRADE GENERAL EDUCATION

As an education major, what changed the game for me was actually teaching. My university did a whole year of student teaching. I'm so thankful because I don't think I would have felt confident enough without that year in the classroom before graduating.

I had my first real moment of *I can do this* when I was student teaching. I was kind of on the edge, thinking, *Will this even happen for me?* My mentor was an amazing teacher, so I figured I would just copy her—fake it till I make it. But in the second half of the year, I started adding in some of my own ideas and trying to add movement and new systems that the class didn't yet have. Once you start figuring out the little elements of your personality that work and you find your systems, it's so encouraging. You realize you have the tools to do this.

For me, classroom songs were a really big turning point. At first, we'd use them as a transition from the carpet to our desks. Later, as I kept teaching and got more creative, I started writing my own songs for learning purposes. I'd write a song about math to help them really grasp the concept. The kids would get so excited—they really owned singing them. It boosted not only our community, but also the energy of our learning experience.

Songs became a big pillar for me. We would start the day with a song all about being our best selves, treating each other the right way, and bringing good energy to the classroom. I made the songs applicable to the subject we were working on, so when we're learning about adjectives, we'd sing the adjective song. Bringing music in really helps make my classroom a little more fun.

★ You realize you have the tools to do this.

I love to create things that make memories for the kids. One example of that is themed learning days. The first one I made was a café day. We'd do all our normal subjects—math, science, reading, language arts—but every activity had a café theme. For math, we worked with a cash register and added customer orders, and in grammar we edited a café menu, looking for spelling and grammatical mistakes. The kids got so excited, so engaged, and it made me want to do more of it. Over the years, I slowly added on, and even though themed days are extra preparation, they really give me energy because the kids get so excited. I always think, *I can't wait for café day.*

To me, the most special part of being a teacher is creating your classroom community. The end of the year can be hard for teachers because you've built this little group that supports each other and cheers each other on every single day. If your classroom is like mine, you might have little catchphrases you say or inside jokes. We've formed all these memories.

With one kiddo who wasn't thriving in school, I made it my mission that this would be their year to love it. I really felt like I succeeded; he started to love coming in every day. Then we found out he had to move early in the school year. He came in so sad, and I was heartbroken because I felt like he had the safety he needed in my classroom and with me. He trusted me and I didn't know if this other school would be the same for him. The transition happened sooner than we expected, and we didn't get a formal goodbye. It was so heartbreaking. Luckily, we got a little closure one day when we discovered what school he went to. I sent his teacher a letter and his grandmother came by to pick up a gift I got for him. She came back at the end of Christmas break and told me, "He misses you so much, but he's doing good." She gave me a letter he'd written back: He said that he missed us, and he was still part of our class family. It was so touching. Even though I don't know all the details of his life, I can kind of let him go. It was just so hard to start that relationship and not get to end it with him how I had pictured.

I write my students a letter at the end of each school year, and I read it to them the second to last week of school, but I can never get through it. All I can think about is this little community I created, and how I have to wish them well into a new year where I don't get to be their person anymore. It's so hard to say goodbye. Hopefully they remember the feeling of walking in and feeling loved and feeling like they were part of something. My goal is always to make them feel connected as a community but also to call out individually what gifts they have and how special they are. You don't get to see exactly where they go or how they grow up, but you hope that the love you poured in is something they can hold on to.

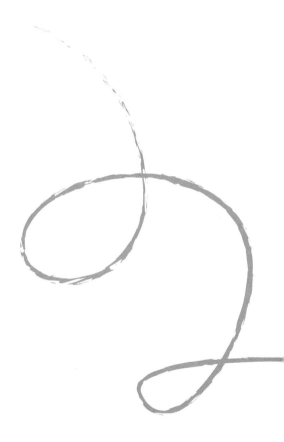

The Importance of Relationships

Mr. Josh Monroe

NEBRASKA

FOURTH GRADE
GENERAL EDUCATION

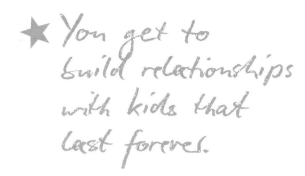

You get to build relationships with kids that last forever.

When I first started teaching, I thought that I'd walk in and kids would learn and do well just because I was fun. I quickly realized that that was a horrible mindset. I did a lot of reading on how to better my classroom management, and everything I read went back to the importance of relationships. Then, once I became a parent, I started to view the world differently, especially teaching.

Behavior is always the most challenging part of the job. It took me a really long time to figure out how to not take it personally. I had to learn what it meant to be a good teacher, and to grow from my first day to where I'm at now has taken a lot of hard work.

It's your job to have a kid throw a chair at you, and then you've still got to love that kid and be there with them and teach them. It's about learning how to let some of those things go and understanding that behavior is a form of communication. You need to think, *What is this kid trying to tell me?*

Behavior is the most challenging part of teaching, but I also think it's the most fun too. You get to build relationships with kids that last forever. That's part of why I like the older elementary grades: it's when kids start to figure out who they are and who they want to be. I like being part of that process.

My dog comes to school with me. Nala is a ten-year-old Westie and a nationally certified therapy dog. She loves coming to school, and the kids love her. It's amazing to watch them build relationships with her. When she first comes in at the beginning of the school year, I tell kids that it's really important that she's not a distraction. If she's going to be part of our class, she's going to add to the environment, not take away from the learning we've got to do.

She's been kids' partners in assignments before. They read to her. Once, a little girl came into class and curled up on the floor crying. I walked over and tried to talk to her, but she told me she wanted to be alone. I said, "Okay," and I honored that and left. And then Nala walked over to the girl, and the girl just hugged Nala for about fifteen minutes. After she let go, she had a great rest of the day. The girl didn't want to talk to me, but whatever happened between them helped.

It's been so special; I've had Nala since she was eight weeks old, and now she's helped hundreds of people. She helps out in more ways than I probably even realize. I've had some pretty high-behavior kids in my class, but when Nala's there, she changes the atmosphere of the room. When she walks in, kids are more relaxed and at ease.

A couple times a week, I give up my plan time and visit other classes around the school with Nala. We get to hang out with kids. At the end of the school year this year, kids were crying and saying, "Nala, I'm gonna miss you so much."

I can't emphasize enough the importance of hanging out with your kids. We all need breaks every once in a while, and planning time and lunch are great for that. But taking the time to go to music or art or PE with them, playing with them at recess, and eating lunch with them is super important to develop those deep, meaningful relationships, and to let kids know that you're invested in them, and you love them. From 8:10 a.m., when that bell rings, until 3:10 p.m., when they leave, my time is for them.

Special Thanks To

Thank you to every extraordinary teacher profiled in this book who made time before school, after school, on nights and weekends, and even on spring and summer breaks to participate in this collection. This book was made in celebration of your incredible hard work and your commitment to your students. You are the true heroes of the story.

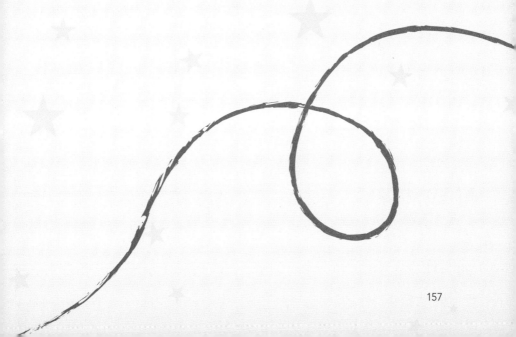

Connect

Many teachers connect with and expand their communities on social media. We have listed the handles of those who wish to share their accounts in this book.

First published in 2025 by Rock Point, an imprint of The Quarto Group,
142 West 36th Street, 4th Floor, New York, NY 10018, USA
(212) 779-4972 www.Quarto.com

Rock Point titles are also available at discount for retail, wholesale, promotional,
and bulk purchase. For details, contact the Special Sales Manager by email at
specialsales@quarto.com or by mail at The Quarto Group, Attn: Special Sales
Manager, 100 Cummings Center Suite 265D, Beverly, MA 01915 USA.

10 9 8 7 6 5 4 3 2 1

ISBN: 978-1-57715-478-5

Digital edition published in 2025
eISBN: 978-0-7603-9301-7

Library of Congress Control Number: 2024948761

Group Publisher: Rage Kindelsperger
Editorial Director: Erin Canning
Creative Director: Laura Drew
Managing Editor: Cara Donaldson
Senior Acquiring Editor: Nicole James
Editor: Katelynn Abraham
Interior Design: Andy Warren Design
Writing Support: L. J. Tracosas

Printed in China

This book provides general information on various widely known and widely
accepted images that tend to evoke feelings of strength and confidence.
However, it should not be relied upon as recommending or promoting any
specific diagnosis or method of treatment for a particular condition, and it is
not intended as a substitute for medical or mental health advice or for direct
diagnosis and treatment of a medical or mental health condition by a qualified
physician. Readers who have questions about a particular condition, possible
treatments for that condition, or possible reactions from the condition or its
treatment should consult a physician or other qualified health care professional.